40 DIGITAL
PHOTOGRAPHY
TECHNIQUES

Y.

ISBN: 89-314-3511-8

Printed and bound in the Republic of Korea.

How to contact us

E-mail: support@youngjin.com
feedback@youngjin.com.sg
Address: Youngjin.com
1623-10, Seocho-dong, Seocho-gu
Seoul 137-878
Korea

Telephone: +65-6327-1161
Fax: +65-6327-1151

Manager: Suzie Lee
Chief Editor: Angelica Lim
Acquisitions and Developmental Editor: Mariann Barsolo
Production Editor: Dennis Fitzgerald
Copyeditor: Nancy Riddiough
Book Designer: Semtle
Cover Designer: Litmus
Production Control: Ann Lee

A Note from the Author

Dear Reader,

Thank you for choosing 40 Digital Photography Techniques, 2nd Edition.

If you are new to digital photography or if you have taken digital images without understanding how a digital camera really works, this book will be great for you. This is because in this book, we will start with an introduction to the digital camera before moving on to its more advanced features. For film camera owners, this book also contains a brief comparison between film and digital cameras to help build on existing knowledge and let you make a smooth transition from film to digital.

As for digital camera owners, this book will show a lot more than what's in the manual. It describes 40 techniques for achieving specific results, using a combination of technical skills, art theories, and traditional photography know-how. Whether you enjoy taking pictures of people, landscape, or any other subject, you will learn all the techniques in this compact little book filled with plenty of examples and ideas. This book will also show you how to transfer, print, and share your images on the Internet.

Because this is a second edition, a number of changes and additions have been made. At the end of every chapter, you will find a checklist that helps you recap what you have learned. The checklists, with topics ranging from general steps for shooting to taking pictures of people, make a great reference and provide a quick refresher course. In particular, the checklist on buying a camera that is right for you will be a great resource. This checklist will help you in choosing a camera necessary for shooting the subject that you are interested in, without buying into the features that you don't really need.

In addition, two new techniques and a special feature on camera phones have been added to this book. You will learn to take wedding photographs and action shots while the special feature on camera phones will keep you up-to-date on the camera feature found on phones. You will find plenty of new images and even more new ideas. We hope that in no time you will discover that you can create fantastic results without using pro cameras. Have fun!

John Kim

Contents

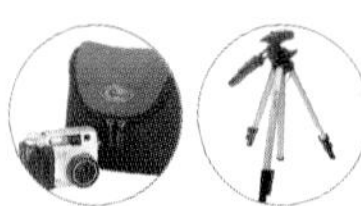

40 Digital Photography Techniques

Getting to Know Your Digital Camera

The first thing I want to do in this book is to help you understand how a digital camera works. As most of you are more familiar with the traditional film camera, I will start by comparing digital cameras to film cameras. Although digital cameras and film cameras are different, they share many similarities.

In this chapter we will also look at the structure and basic functions of a digital camera, and how to choose and accessorize one. So, whether you just bought your first digital camera or are planning an upgrade, this chapter contains the essential information you need.

I Comparing a Digital Camera to a Film Camera

Photography has been around a long time. The first photograph was made in 1826 and there have been many technological advances to produce smaller and better film cameras since. But these advances were incremental; with the invention of the digital camera we witnessed the first photography revolution, making the leap from film to digital in the last century.

The Key Difference

The following figures show you how film and digital cameras record images. As you can see, the two diagrams are nearly identical. The only difference is that light entering a digital camera hits the CCD (Charge-Coupled Device) rather than film. As I mentioned earlier, a film camera and a digital camera share many similarities, so if you know how to use a film camera, you will have no problem operating a digital one.

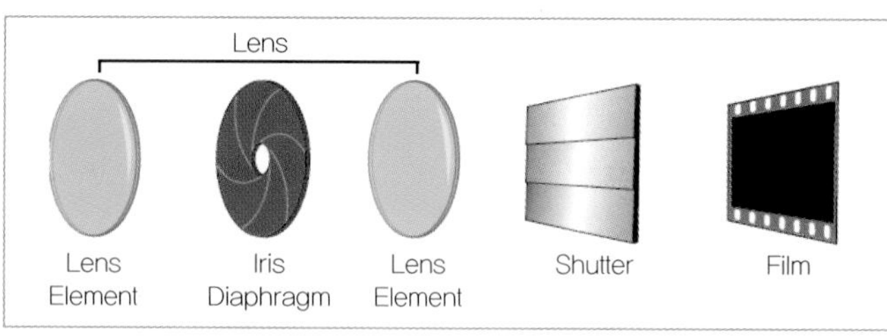

▲ Film camera

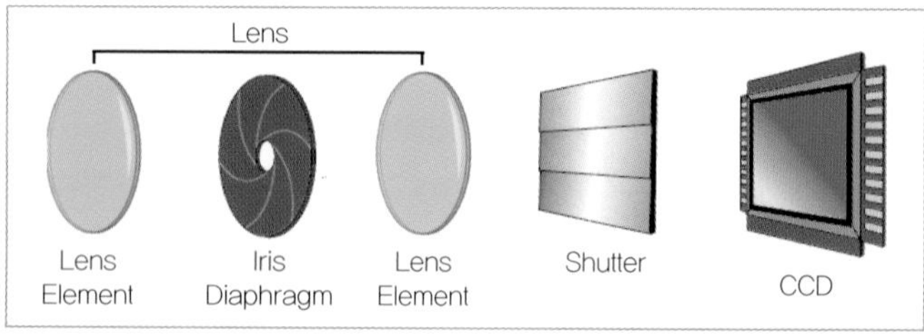

▲ Digital camera

About the CCD (Charge-Coupled Device)

The CCD found in a digital camera is a light-sensitive semiconductor composed of millions of tiny dots known as pixels (short for picture elements). A 4.0-megapixel camera, for instance, has a CCD that comprises 4,000,000 pixels. When light hits the CCD, each pixel is converted into an electrical charge that corresponds to a color in the color spectrum. On the other hand, the film used in traditional cameras is a light-sensitive emulsion that records images through a chemical reaction.

▶ CCD

CMOS (Complementary Metal Oxide Semiconductor)

Some digital cameras use a CMOS (pronounced see-moss) instead of a CCD. As the technical difference between the two is too advanced (and too dry) for this book, all you need to know is that the CMOS records images in the same way as the CCD.

Digital Camera Advantages and Disadvantages

Advantages of the Digital Camera	Disadvantages of the Digital Camera
No need for film.	A digital camera is more expensive than a film camera that produces similar results.
Minimize mistakes. • You can check your photos right after you take them and try again.	Higher energy consumption. • Battery drains more quickly, especially in cold weather.
No need for scanner. • You can transfer digital photos directly to a computer without losing quality. • You can share your photos through e-mail or on the Internet easily.	Time delay. • Startup delay. A digital camera takes longer to start up. • Image capture delay. After taking a shot, some digital cameras will take up to a few seconds to record the image. As it records, you can't take another shot. This can be a problem for action shots.
Flexible printing costs. • You can choose to print only the best images.	There's a limit to the image size you can develop.
It is easier to store, organize, and search for photos.	Poor lighting will produce noise (unwanted specks, grain, etc.) in the image.
The quality of the photos won't degrade with time or as additional copies are made.	The product life cycle is very short, so finding compatible accessories can be a problem if the camera has been on the market for awhile.

Other Advantages of the Digital Camera

One of the best things about digital cameras is their small size. Digital cameras can be made smaller than film cameras because the CCD is smaller than a roll of film. Because of this, there is a trend to equip laptops, cell phones, MP3 players, and even watches with small and compact digital cameras.

Another advantage of the digital camera is that it can be easily coupled with other electronic products since it is a digital device itself. The most popular combination is between digital cameras and camcorders. You can take still shots with digital camcorders or record movies with a digital camera. The camcorder feature in most digital cameras lets you shoot anywhere from three-second to three-minute movies. However, some of the latest digital cameras are equipped with full camcorder functionality.

▲ Canon PowerShot A80 (digital camera)

II Structure and Basic Functions

Before you can shoot good photos, you need to know your camera well. It always surprises me that so many people shoot photographs without first understanding the capabilities or limitations of their equipment. They sometimes underestimate or try to stretch their camera's capabilities.

Main Features

Refer to your camera manual as you read this book, especially the specifications page.

▶▶▶ CCD

Many novice photographers think that the number of pixels on the CCD is the only factor to consider in terms of picture quality. The size of the CCD is just as important. What we are seeing on the market now are digital cameras with even more pixels, while the size of the CCD itself remains pretty much the same.

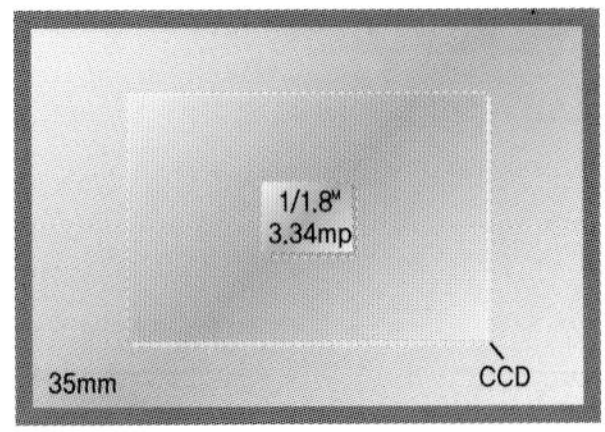

▲ Comparing the size of the CCD on a consumer camera (1/1.8″) with the CCD on a high-end camera and a 35mm film

The reason for this phenomenon is that the CCD is the most expensive element in a digital camera and increasing its size will increase costs significantly. Since CCDs are costly, many companies try to squeeze more pixels into CCDs to reduce costs. But this causes pixels to overlap, lowering the quality of individual pixels and creating a lot of noise. This is why bigger CCDs are found only in a few high-end digital cameras and manufacturers push their cameras along the megapixel line.

As a guide, look for cameras with a CCD that is at least 1/1.8 inches with more than 2.0 megapixels.

▶▶▶ File Formats

When saving images on a digital camera, you will be asked to choose a file format. Here's a run-down of the formats available:

- JPEG: JPEG (Joint Photographic Experts Group) is the name of the organization that developed this file format. One of the biggest advantages of JPEG is that it can compress image data at a ratio of 20:1 or higher, resulting in small file sizes that are great for the Web. The downside of this popular format is that it uses a lossy compression scheme: It throws away image data during compression. Therefore, each time you open and resave as a JPEG, some data gets lost and the image degrades further.

- TIFF: This is another popular file format. When saving as a TIFF, you can select no compression to maintain image quality or LZW compression, which is a lossless compression scheme, to minimize damage. Although the difference in quality between JPEG and TIFF images cannot be seen on the small LCD monitor, it becomes obvious when the images are printed. The no-compression TIFF format is a better choice for printing, but it does not create small file sizes like JPEG.

- RAW: As the name implies, the RAW file format saves images in their raw, unprocessed form. Images are saved in this format on the camera before they are saved as JPEG or TIFF.

tip Most entry-level cameras support only JPEG, while average to high-end cameras support JPEG and TIFF or JPEG and RAW.

▶▶▶ Image Resolution

This refers to the image size in pixels. The average range is from 640 × 480 pixels to 2272 × 1704 pixels. Most cameras support a few sizes, and it is a good idea to buy a camera with more choices (such as higher resolution). However, remember that the larger the pixel size, the bigger the file size.

▶▶▶ JPEG Compression Levels

Choose from Super-Fine, Fine, or Normal compression levels when taking photos in JPEG format. Most photographers set compression to Super Fine (the lowest compression rate) for better image quality. However, you should note that a low compression rate produces a bigger file size.

▶▶▶ Lens

The lens used in a camera is a major factor in determining camera quality and price. Leading camera manufacturers, such as Nikon, Canon, and Olympus, use their own lenses in their cameras. Other brands, like Sony, Casio, and Panasonic, use third-party lenses.

▲ Leica is a renowned lens maker whose lens are often used in cameras other than their own.

What Is Focal Length?

The focal length of a lens is the distance between the lens and the point where the incoming light rays focus behind the lens. The focal length is measured in millimeters. If the lens length is not fixed (a zoom lens, for example), you will see the focal length expressed as a range in the camera's specifications. A short focal length is used when zooming out to wide-angle shots while a long focal length is used when zooming in on subjects for close-ups (telephoto).

What Is 35mm Camera Equivalent?

In your camera's specifications, you will probably see the words *35mm film equivalent* followed by your camera's focal length range. This means that a lens with a focal length of 7.1mm to 21.3mm on a digital camera, for example, will produce results that are equivalent to a lens with a focal length of 35mm to 105mm on a 35mm film camera.

▶▶▶ Zoom

In general, digital cameras support two different types of zooms: optical zoom and digital zoom. Optical zoom is achieved by using the camera lens while digital zoom works by taking a part of an image that has been shot and enlarging it. Digital zoom works in the same way as the zoom tool in graphics programs such as Photoshop Elements. Every time you use digital zoom, the resolution of the image goes down. In contrast, there's no loss of resolution when you use optical zoom. The digital zoom function is of little use most of the time, so beware of advertising hype that focuses on the digital zoom capability.

▲ Nikon CoolPix 5400: 4X optical zoom lens

▶▶▶ Focusing Range

This refers to the range within which the camera can focus on a subject. Most cameras can focus to a distance of infinity, so the main concern is how close the camera can focus. This factor determines if you can take extremely close shots of small objects such as flowers or insects. Most cameras can focus from the minimum distance of 1 cm to 10 cm.

▶▶▶ Aperture

Behind the lens is an iris diaphragm (illustrated on page 8). Adjusting the size of its opening controls the amount of light passing through to the CCD. The size of this opening is the aperture. The iris diaphragm is so called because its overlapping blades work like the iris of the eye.

▶▶▶ Shutter Speed

For film cameras, this refers to the length of time the shutter stays open to let light into the camera. Most digital cameras, however, do not actually use a physical shutter to control exposure time. They use an electronic switch to tell the camera how long to keep the CCD turned on. Shutter speed is measured in fractions of a second.

▶▶▶ Exposure Control

Exposure refers to the amount of light that the CCD or film receives for a shot. Two factors control the exposure of an image: shutter speed and aperture. If you have an automatic camera, the camera will set the exposure automatically for you. Depending on your camera, you may have the exposure compensation feature, which lets you modify the exposure automatically set by the camera. Some automatic cameras also have Scene modes—a set of pre-programmed settings recommended for specific situations.

For semiautomatic or manual cameras, you have more control because these cameras have Shutter Priority, Aperture Priority, or Manual modes. In Shutter Priority mode, you set the shutter speed and the camera chooses the aperture setting. It's the other way around in the Aperture Priority mode. In Manual mode, you set both the shutter speed and aperture.

▶▶▶ Sensitivity

This refers to the sensitivity of the CCD when it receives light and is rated in ISO. A low ISO rating means that it is less sensitive and needs more light to expose an image properly. When you shoot a subject at ISO 100 or lower, your image will look softer. Conversely, a high ISO means that you will need less light. Unfortunately, a raised ISO rating only boosts the electronic signal from the shot and this can create graininess in your images. The most common ISO ratings are from ISO 100 to ISO 400, but high-end cameras can have a rating of up to ISO 3200.

▶▶▶ Flash

The built-in flash that comes with a digital camera can usually light up to a distance of 9–10 feet (3 meters). Some digital cameras use an infrared sensor to determine the distance between the camera and the subject and adjust the flash intensity according to that information. Check your user's manual to find out the exact flash coverage. It is important to know this to illuminate your objects properly.

▶▶▶ Continuous Shot Function

This feature, which is found in most digital cameras, enables you to take a few continuous shots by pressing the shutter release button only once.

▲ Consecutive images taken with the Continuous Shot function

▶▶▶ Movies

Except for a few high-priced cameras, most digital cameras can only record a 30-second movie when the image resolution is set to 640x480 pixels. If the image resolution is lowered to 320×240 pixels, you can record for about three minutes.

▶▶▶ Viewfinder/LCD Monitor

One common problem with using the viewfinder is parallax error. This is because the viewfinder shows the image from a viewpoint that is slightly different than what is actually captured on the CCD. As the problem usually occurs while shooting close-ups, you should use the LCD (liquid crystal display) when shooting at close range. The LCD shows you the camera settings being used and a preview of the image. You can also review images that have been taken.

▶▶▶ Storage Media

The most common and popular choice for storage is a CompactFlash (CF) card, which can store up to 12GB of data. On cameras that support the Type II CF card, a microdrive that has a capacity of up to 4GB can be used. Other memory cards include Sony's Memory Stick, which, unfortunately, can only be used with Sony cameras and some Samsung cameras. It is also more expensive.

At the time I am writing this book, the SD and xD-Picture cards are getting a lot of good reviews. These cards are being hailed as the "memory cards of the future" because their physical size is getting smaller, even as their memory capacity gets bigger. It does not really matter which storage media you choose. Check that you have at least 32MB of memory. Even with 32MB of memory you can only store about 40 images at a resolution of 3.2 megapixels in JPEG format.

▲ 512MB CompactFlash card

▲ HITACHI 2GB microdrive

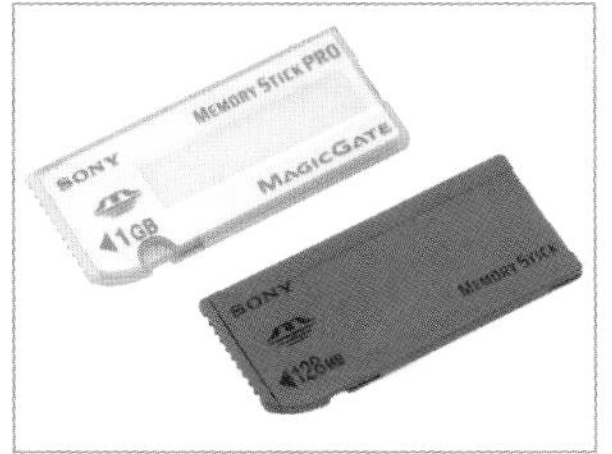

▲ Sony's Memory Stick

▲ The SD and xD-Picture cards

▶▶▶ Power Sources

A digital camera is composed of many electronic parts. These parts, coupled with a frequent use of the LCD monitor, can drain the camera's batteries very quickly. The problem is even more acute in cold weather.

The current trend is to create digital cameras that use only rechargeable lithium ion batteries. These batteries are long lasting by digital camera standards, but they are also more expensive. However, there are some cameras out on the market that use both lithium and alkaline batteries. With such cameras, you can use alkaline batteries when the lithium ones fail.

▲ Olympus's lithium ion battery pack and charger

▶▶▶ Dimensions and Weight

A small and light digital camera is obviously the first choice for portability. However, it can be difficult to hold such cameras steady while taking pictures, and you could end up with blurry images.

Ⅲ

Choosing the Right Digital Camera

Now that you know what makes up a digital camera and how it works, let's look at choosing the right camera. Even if you already have a digital camera, the information in this section could help you in making your next purchase. Three of the most important factors in purchasing a camera are cost, portability, and needs. Of course, if you have a huge budget, you can get a top-of-the-line camera. However, high-end cameras are usually heavy and not very portable. This is why you should also consider your needs.

Automatic Cameras

Most fully automatic digital cameras have a resolution of around 1.0 to 3.0 megapixels and no manual exposure control. The camera determines the settings for you automatically, so all you need to do is to press the shutter release button.

Other cameras that fall into the automatic digital camera category are new models that have Scene modes such as the Portrait mode. Each of these modes is a collection of pre-programmed settings that are suitable for specific kinds of shots.

▲ Nikon Coolpix 3200

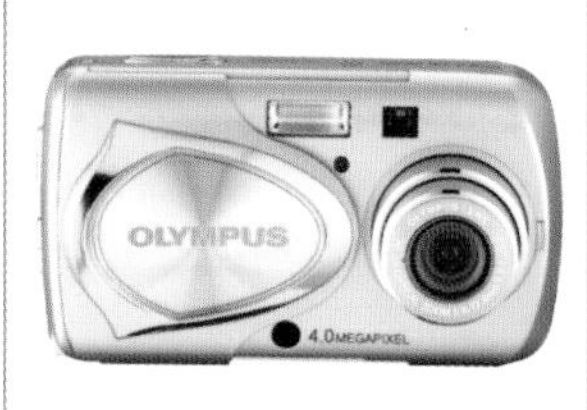

▲ Olympus Stylus 410

Semiautomatic and Manual Cameras

Such digital cameras usually have a resolution between 3.0 and 6.0 megapixels and allow you to manually set exposure and focus. You will find Shutter Priority, Aperture Priority, and Manual modes on these cameras.

▲ Olympus C-8080 Wide Zoom

▲ Canon PowerShot Pro-1

tip Prices for digital cameras have fallen recently, so I would recommend that beginners buy a camera in this category. Once you have some control over exposure, you can take better and more creative pictures.

SLR Digital Cameras

SLR (single-lens reflex) cameras are top-of-the-line cameras used by professionals and have a resolution ranging from 3.0 to 14.0 megapixels. Other than manual controls, one of the best things about these cameras is that you can change and use a variety of different lenses. These cameras are expensive and not really necessary for photography hobbyists.

▲ Canon EOS 1D Mark 2

▲ Nikon D70

Grip Cameras

Cameras with grips are gaining popularity as they are easier to hold steady, especially if the camera is heavy. However, this is largely a matter of personal taste. There are some who think that such cameras don't feel right in their hands. The best way to find out if you will like such a camera is to try it at the store.

▲ Konica Minolta DiMAGE A2

Special Cameras

▲ Sony Cybershot U20

There are tiny cameras on the market that are extremely portable. But they also have very low resolution, so you may end up with images that you can't print at a decent size.

tip How Many Pixels Do You need?

As a general guide, you need a resolution of 300 pixels per inch for photographic quality prints. If, for example, you want to print your images at 4R (4 x 6), you should preferably have a resolution of 1,200 (i.e. 4 x 300) x 1,800 (i.e. 6 x 300) or 2.2 megapixels.

If you enjoy taking pictures of yourself and your companions, a camera with a rotating lens or LCD is a must. Just rotate the lens or LCD 180° to point at yourself, check your image in the LCD, and click. Such cameras are also great for making overhead or tight shots.

▲ Nikon Coolpix SQ with rotating lens

▲ Canon Powershot G-5 with rotating LCD

tip Faulty Pixels

Always check that the camera does not produce faulty pixels. There are two kinds of bad pixels: dead and hot pixels. Dead pixels, like the name suggests, are no longer working and are, therefore, black. Hot pixels, on the other hand, receive the wrong electronic signals, leading to the display of white or other color pixels.

The problem can be with either the LCD or CCD. You can check the LCD visually to see if it is responding to the electronic signals correctly. The problem is more serious if the camera has a faulty CCD that's sending the wrong signals. This is because a faulty LCD does not affect the picture but a faulty CCD does. If you have already bought the camera, ask for a replacement. Although different manufacturers have different exchange policies, most would let you exchange the CCD at least twice and the LCD at least three times.

▲ A faulty LCD can be detected right away.

IV Accessorizing Your Digital Camera

Once you start taking photos you will begin seeing photo opportunities in many different locations and situations—some of which can be rather challenging. There are many accessories that will help you take better pictures or at least make the process easier, but unnecessary items will only weigh you down. Having said that, let's take a look at some common accessories.

Essential Accessories

▶▶▶ Memory Card

Top on the list is an additional memory card. Most digital cameras come with an 8MB to 32MB memory card. However, you will soon find that this is insufficient and I would recommend that you buy an additional 128MB to 256MB memory card.

▲ 256MB card

▶▶▶ Battery

It is very likely that you may drain your battery while shooting outdoors, so it is advisable to have a reserve battery on hand. If the camera comes with a non-rechargeable battery, you should consider buying a rechargeable battery pack and a rapid charger, which will be more cost-effective and convenient in the long run.

▲ Rapid charger

▶▶▶ Tripod

Although the tripod is an important camera accessory, many avoid using it because it is cumbersome. Tripods are commonly used for taking portraits and shots in low-light conditions, such as at night, and indoor shots so as to prevent camera shake. Get a light yet sturdy tripod, and if you are worried about bulkiness, get a mini-tripod.

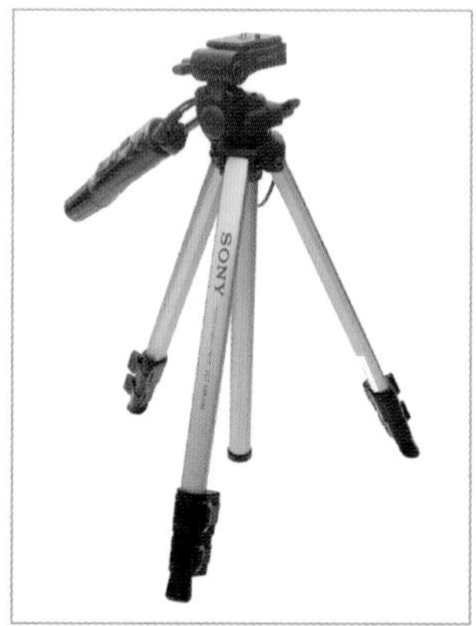

▲ Sony's basic tripod

▲ Mini-tripod

▶▶▶ Camera Bag

Although a portable bag comes with the camera, it is better to buy a padded one for greater shock absorption. In addition, consider buying a waterproof camera bag or one that has a waterproof cover for those rainy days.

▲ Lowepro's digital camera bag

Other Accessories

▶▶▶ Filter

Generally speaking, you can attach filters to your lens to create special effects if you have a mid- to high-end digital camera. Even though Photoshop Elements can create these effects easily, some photographers prefer to use filters so that they can visualize the results in the viewfinder. Some of the filters available are polarizing filters, color-warming filters, and star filters.

▲ UV filters correct for ultraviolet light, which can result in a bluish cast.

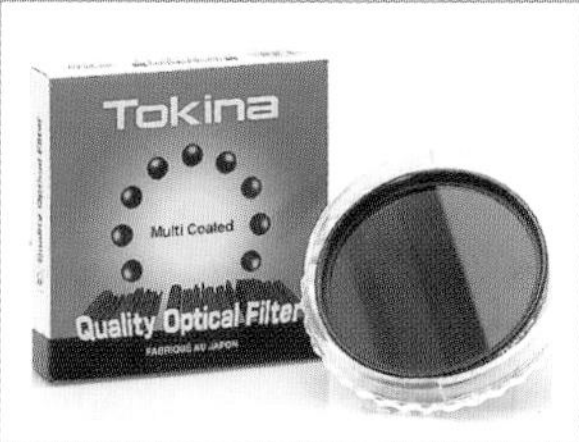

▲ Polarizing filters eliminate surface reflections and enhance tint contrast.

▶▶▶ Conversion Lens

This is placed over the camera's fixed lens to create a variety of effects. Some conversion lenses include the wide-angle conversion lens and the telephoto conversion lens.

▶ Conversion lenses

▶▶▶ Lens Adapter

You may need a lens adapter to attach a filter or conversion lens.

▶ Olympus lens adapter

▶▶▶ Card Reader

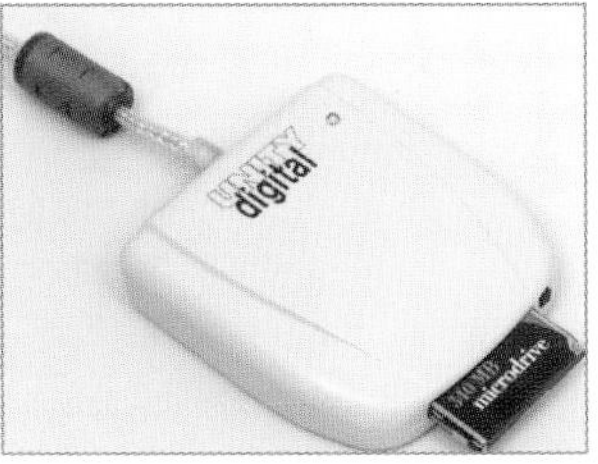

▲ Using the card reader to transmit pictures

Although you can transfer images from your digital camera to the computer via the USB cable, this transferral method will drain the batteries of your camera and you can't use your camera while it is transferring images. A more convenient method is to use a card reader. If you have a number of devices, such as a PDA (personal digital assistant), that use storage media cards, you should get a multiple card reader that will read a variety of cards.

First, connect the card reader to your camera's USB port and then insert a memory card into the reader. Next, connect the card reader to the computer. The computer will think of the card reader as just another external cache, allowing you to transmit your pictures easily.

▶▶▶ External Flash

Most digital cameras come with a small, built-in flash. However, there may be times when the built-in flash is not bright enough, and you may need to use an external flash, or strobe. Some cameras have a hot shoe to which you can connect the strobe.

▲ The hot shoe

▲ Strobe connected to the hot shoe

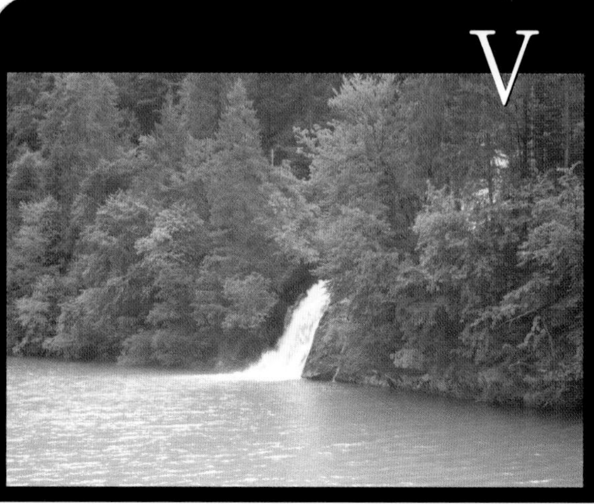

V Camera Care

A digital camera is a sophisticated device made up of very small, sensitive electronic components. So even minute particles like dust, moisture, and salt can damage your camera and render it useless. On one hand, it is important that you keep your camera clean and free from harmful particles. On the other hand, excessive cleaning can damage its parts. Since neither excessive nor inadequate care is desirable, let's learn to provide the right level of care in this section.

Dusting the Camera

Before and after using a camera, use the blower (air brush) to remove dust. If the blower is not effective, use a soft brush or a lens pen. Fingerprints and other foreign matter on the lens can be removed gently using a lens cleaning cloth. Because lenses have a multi-layer coating on the surface for reducing internal reflection, you need to clean gently since excessive rubbing or wiping can wear the coating out. Unless absolutely necessary, you should refrain from touching the lens in any way. A little dust on the lens will generally not affect your photos, so don't worry about it too much.

▲ Blower

Removing Excess Moisture

Always store your camera in a cool, dry place—preferably with some desiccant. You should never store your camera in direct sunlight. As I have mentioned before, mold can form on camera lenses left in humid conditions. Once in a while, you should take your camera out of storage to air it. The best thing to do is to use your camera every day.

▲ Lens brush and lens cloth

Cleaning the Lens

Frequent cleaning is not desirable as this can wear off the anti-reflective coating on the lens. If you must clean the lens, follow these steps:

▶▶▶ Using the Blower

Blowing on the lens with your breath can get saliva and condensation on the lens, which is why it is recommended that you use a blower. In most cases, this is all you need to do to clean and take care of the lens.

▶ Using the blower

▶▶▶ Using the Lens Brush

Sometimes there are a few stubborn specks of dirt that refuse to budge when using the blower. In such cases, you can use a soft lens brush.

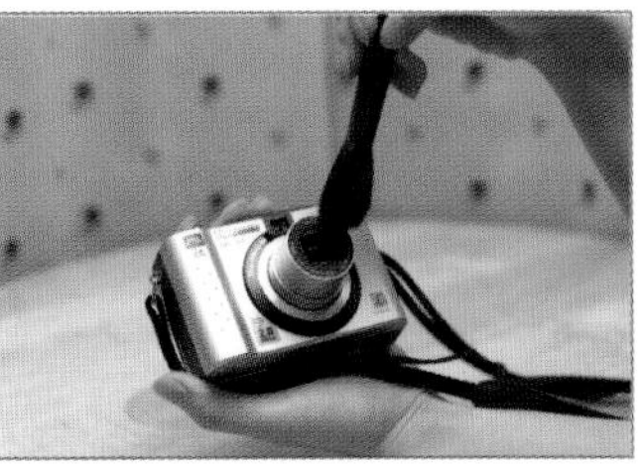

▶ Using the lens brush

▶▶▶ Using the Lens Cloth

To remove fingerprints and other foreign matter from the lens, wrap a lens cloth lightly around your finger and gently wipe the lens, using a circular motion. If this doesn't work, take your camera to the nearest service center.

▶ Using the lens cloth

Watch Where You Place Your Fingers!

Our fingers have small traces of perspiration on them, which is why touching a lens leaves behind small amounts of moisture and salt residue. You should, therefore, always know where you place your fingers when using the digital camera.

Camera Care Under Other Situations

▶▶▶ At the Beach

Sea air contains salt particles, which is a no-no for a digital camera. The salt will cling to the digital camera, both inside and out, causing corrosion. Should this happen, use a slightly damp cloth to wipe off the salt residue from the outside of the camera and then go over it again using a camera cloth. It's best to avoid exposing your camera to sea air for long periods of time.

▶▶▶ If Your Camera Gets Wet

A wet digital camera can be dangerous. You should remove the battery before you do anything else. Do not switch on the camera in an attempt to see if it is broken. Use a cloth to wipe the water off the camera body and take it immediately to a nearby service center. If you drop your camera in the sea, rinse the camera with drinking water to remove the salt residue before taking the camera in for repairs.

▶▶▶ In Winter

As I have said before, the camera's battery drains quickly at low temperatures. If you keep the battery warm before using it (by keeping it in your pocket, for example), you can extend the battery life. Another problem is water condensation. If you bring your camera indoors after using it out in the cold, water will condense on both the outside and inside of the camera. To prevent this from happening, place the camera in its bag before bringing it inside. This allows the camera to gradually adjust to the higher room temperature.

c h e c k l i s t

Checklist: Buying a Digital Camera

√ For both urban and rural landscapes, you will need a wide-angle lens or a conversion lens (35 mm or wider film equivalent, preferably 28mm) in order to fit the entire scene into your picture.

√ To take photographs of objects that you cannot approach, such as wild animals, you will need a camera lens with six times optical zoom (i.e., 35mm–210mm or longer). Alternatively, you can buy a telephoto conversion lens to beef up an existing camera's telephoto capability.

√ If you take many indoor shots, the manual white balance feature is useful for removing the color cast from indoor lighting.

√ For indoor pictures of a group of people standing, you will need an external flash gun or strobe that can illuminate up to 13 feet (4 meters) or farther. You should first check if your camera has a hot shoe to which you can attach the external flash unit.

√ To capture a freeze frame of fast-moving subjects such as toddlers, you will need an automatic camera with a Sports Scene mode at the very least. For really fast-moving objects such as cars and athletics at sporting events, you will need a camera with very large aperture (f/2.8 to f/2.0) and a fast shutter speed (1/250 second or faster). To consistently take good action shots, you will at least need a semiautomatic camera that will let you set the shutter speed. You should note that it is hard to take action shots with automatic cameras (lower your expectation!).

√ For self-portraits, a rotating lens or LCD will let you compose and take pictures of yourself without having to ask someone else to take the shot.

√ To shoot close-ups of small objects such as insects and flowers, look for a camera with a minimum focusing distance of 4cm or less.

√ It is a good idea to buy an additional memory card. As a guide, if your camera has a resolution of 4.0 megapixels, you should consider getting a 256MB memory card (stores approximately 140 images).

√ To take pictures of a city at night, you will need a tripod and a cable release or a camera with a remote control. This will keep the camera steady during long exposures.

√ For shots of the beach, snow, or sky, you will need a camera with a Beach or Snow Scene mode, the exposure compensation feature, or the ability to adjust exposure manually.

√ The product life cycle for most cameras is two years, so don't overbuy. To print an 8R photo, you will only need a camera with a resolution of 4.0 megapixels. For beginners, it is best to start with an affordable automatic or semiautomatic camera before moving on to pricier cameras. After you've had some experience with photography, you will know the type of photographs you are likely to take and can then decide on whether you need certain camera features.

40 Digital Photography Techniques

Chapter 1

The Basics of Taking Photos

I cannot emphasize enough the need to learn the right techniques from the start. In any field of study, using the wrong technique is the same as, if not worse than, not knowing anything at all. So in this chapter, we will look at such basics as preparing for a shoot, taking care of a digital camera, holding a camera and good posture, adjusting image size, using lenses, locking a focus, controlling exposure, and composing an image.

Chapter 1

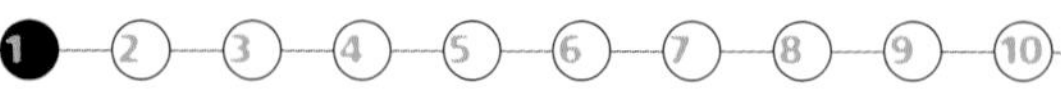

1 Preparing to Shoot

The only way you will take better photos is with practice. To get enough practice, you must always have the camera by your side. The camera has to be kept in top working condition so that you won't miss a practice opportunity or ruin any shots. Before you run out the door with your camera, let's go over some pre-shoot checks in this section.

Gather Your Equipment

First of all, you need to get the battery ready because the digital camera is an energy guzzler. If you are using a rechargeable battery, you will need to charge the battery to full power. This will probably take about two hours. If you are using regular alkaline batteries, take some extras along.

▲ Get in the habit of charging your batteries.

Next, check that the lens is clean and that there is nothing physically wrong with the camera. Also make sure that you have inserted the memory card. People who use a memory card reader often forget that they have left their cards in the reader. They get everything else ready and then head outside with a digital camera that has no memory.

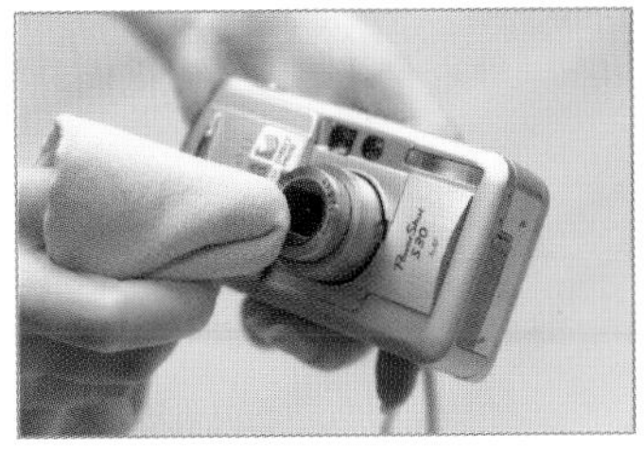
▲ If the lens is dirty, clean it gently.

▲ Make sure that the memory card is in the camera.

▲ Check that the camera straps are not loose.

Finally, check that the camera straps are secure. If not, you run the risk of dropping and breaking your camera.

When you have completed the checks, it is time to pack your equipment (camera, lens cleaning cloth, blower, extra memory card, mini-tripod, and so on) into the camera bag. It is a good idea to include a desiccant so as to absorb excess moisture and keep your equipment dry. Your lens will get moldy and the electronic parts will malfunction if your camera is kept in a humid environment.

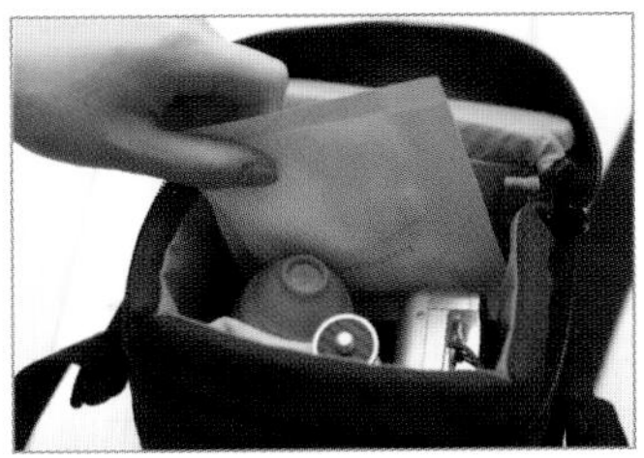
▲ Professional photographers keep their equipment in a dry box but for hobbyists, a desiccant will do.

Planning the Shoot

Before you start shooting, think about the photos you are going to take, and be specific. Instead of stopping at "I'm going to take a photo of my family today," think about how and what kind of family photos you want to take. When you have a plan, you are less likely to miss golden moments.

Most people take more pictures when they use a digital rather than a film camera. Because of this you may end up taking many similar shots, and few meaningful ones, if you don't have an action plan in mind.

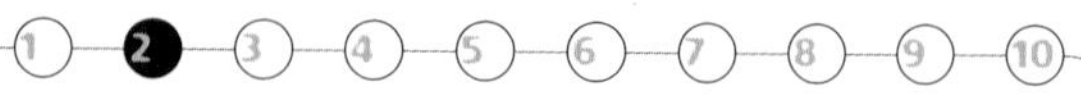

Preventing Camera Shake and Blurring

The secret to non-fuzzy photos lies in your grip and stance. Knowing how to hold and stand with a camera is important in combating even the slightest camera shake, so the first thing I will do in this secion is introduce the correct techniques. After that, we will look at how you can adjust your camera's settings to reduce blur and snap sharper images.

Getting Familiar with the Camera

Most people hold their camera with the left hand and use the right hand to press the shutter and adjust other functions. There are many buttons on the back of the digital camera, but you will probably use only a few of them.

Check your camera's manual to get familiar with the buttons, and remember to press them lightly but firmly.

▲ Familiarize yourself with the buttons and functions on your camera.

▲ Hold the camera steady and press the shutter lightly.

Getting a Good Grip

Place your left palm at the base of the camera. Use your right hand to hold the camera, or the grip, and place your right index finger lightly on the shutter. Exert a stronger grip with your left hand. If you hold the camera with a strong right-hand grip, you may move the camera when you press the shutter button. One reminder, though: always keep your fingers clear of the flash, autofocus window, and lens.

▲ Put one hand through the camera strap's loop and rotate your wrist to wrap it around for a safe grip.

▲ For cameras with grips, use your right hand to hold the grip and your left hand to support the base of the lens lightly.

▲ For cameras without grips, use your left palm to support the camera.

▲ If you are using a large lens, use your left hand to hold the lens.

Practicing the Right Stance

Adopting the right stance can prevent blurring the image, lower the risk of dropping the camera, and reduce fatigue during long photography sessions.

▲ Basic stance—keep both arms close to your body and spread your legs shoulder-width apart for balance.

▲ Horizontal photos—keep both arms close to your body.

▲ Vertical photos—make sure your fingers do not cover the lens or the built-in flash.

▲ When taking photos of subjects lower than you, squat down to their level and use your knees to support yourself.

Trying Other Positions

If you are sitting down, raise one knee and use it to support your elbow. If you need to get even lower to take the photo, sit cross-legged on the ground and support your elbows on your knees.

▲ Keep your back straight and your arms close to your body.

▲ Raise one knee and use it to support your upper body.

▲ Sit cross-legged to take low shots.

Using the LCD

When you use the LCD, the camera is held away from your body. Because the camera does not have the added support of your body to help stabilize it, blur becomes a bigger issue.

The LCD stance: Use your left hand to support the camera and your right hand to press the shutter. You should not grip the camera too tightly. In addition, keep the camera as close to your body as possible and tuck your elbows in for more support.

When taking vertical shots through the LCD, check that your fingers are not covering the built-in flash. You probably won't make the mistake of covering the lens with your hand because, if you do, you will see it on the LCD. This is one advantage of using the LCD rather than the viewfinder.

▲ Horizontal frame

▲ Vertical shots—make sure your photo is level.

Regulating Your Breathing

Hold your breath as you press the shutter button, as the subtle movements of your breathing can produce blur in your photos. You should also get into the habit of pausing slightly after shooting an image, as moving immediately after releasing the shutter can also blur your pictures.

Using Objects for Support

One of the best ways to prevent camera shake is to use a tripod, but if you find it troublesome to carry one, you can use other objects at the shoot location for support. This technique is useful for preventing blur when you use a shutter speed of up to 1/20 second.

▲ Using other objects as a substitute tripod

▲ Using the wall

Using a tripod

Sometimes there are no objects on location that you can use for support. To be sure that you get sharp images all of the time, use a tripod.

▲ A proper stance and the use of a tripod are essential for preventing motion blur in photos.

Other Ways of Reducing Blur

▶▶▶ Shutter Speed

A fast shutter speed will diminish blur and appear to freeze action while a slow shutter speed will capture even the slightest movement as blurred streaks. If you are using an automatic camera, you should note that some of the Scene modes, such as Night Landscape and Fireworks Show, use slow shutter speeds and are more prone to blur. When using such Scene modes, it is best to use a tripod or some form of support, as camera shake becomes more obvious.

▶▶▶ Flash

When synched to work with the shutter, the flash can also reduce blur and appear to freeze action. This option is not available on most automatic cameras.

▶▶▶ Lens Type

When you use a telephoto lens (i.e., to zoom in), a slight camera movement will translate into a huge blur in the image because you are zooming in on a small section of the view. The same amount of camera movement will be less obvious when using a wide-angle lens. If you have a semiautomatic camera, you can set a fast shutter speed when using telephoto lenses to combat blur. With an automatic, you should keep your camera steady using an external support.

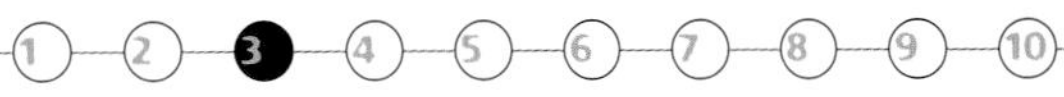

3 Adjusting Image Size and Quality

Unlike a film camera, a digital camera lets you change the size and resolution of your photos as you take them. Surprisingly, not many users know how to use these features to their advantage. Therefore, in this section, we will take the time to learn about image sizes and resolutions.

Image Size or Resolution

Image size and *image resolution* mean the same thing on a digital camera. An image resolution of 1600 x 1200, for example, means that the image is recorded with 1600 pixels across the width and 1200 pixels down the length. So a photo shot with a bigger image size is recorded with more pixels and will print at a better quality.

▶▶▶ Pixels and Maximum Image Size

The maximum image size you can take with your digital camera depends on the number of pixels your camera has, as outlined in the following table:

Pixels	Maximum Image Size
2.0 million	1600 × 1200
4.0 million	2272 × 1704
6.5 million	3072 × 2048

▲ Resolution: 1600 x 1200; file size: 1119KB

▲ Resolution: 800 x 600; file size: 434KB

▲ Resolution: 400 x 300; file size: 134KB

▶▶▶ When Do You Need High-Resolution Images?

Before taking large or high-resolution images, you should consider the capacity of your memory card as these images take up more memory and limit the number of photos you can take. However, there are some instances when you should take high-resolution images. Here are some of them:

- If you need to develop photos that are 8 x 10 or larger.
- If you need to take a close-up but your camera's zoom cannot work at that distance. In such a scenario, you can shoot a high-resolution image, use the crop tool in a graphics program to crop it to size, and blow it up to look like a close-up.

▶▶▶ When Can You Take Low-Resolution Images?

Generally, it is a much better idea to take images at high resolutions and scale them down later than to take low-resolution shots up front. But if quality is not a major concern and quantity is, then these are some situations when you may wish to use low resolution:

- If you have limited memory, as low-resolution images require less memory.
- If you are taking photos for the Internet, you can take images at 800 × 600 pixels or less. Since you need fast downloading speed, you should keep image resolution small.

Using the Continuous Function

When you take continuous shots using the Continuous function, the images are stored temporarily in the camera's buffer memory, which is small in most popular digital camera brands. Therefore, only low-resolution images are taken with the Continuous function.

Image Quality

Images are compressed as they are saved on the memory card in order to reduce the memory they use. The file format used is JPEG, which uses a lossy compression method as I mentioned before. Most cameras usually offer two (Basic or Fine) or three (Normal, Fine, or Super Fine) different levels of image quality. When you set a high image quality (Super Fine), the camera will use a low rate of compression. On the other hand, a high rate of compression creates a low image quality (Basic).

▲ Image resolution: 1600 × 1200; image quality: Normal

▲ Image resolution: 1600 × 1200; image quality: Fine

▲ Image resolution: 1600 × 1200; image quality: Super Fine

Ⓥ Changing Image Size and Quality

In most cameras, you press the Menu button to change the image size and quality. The figures on the right show you how to change the image size and set the image quality to Super Fine. As every camera model is different, the best thing to do is to refer to the manual.

▲ This camera offers four different image sizes to choose from.

▲ This camera has three levels of image guality.

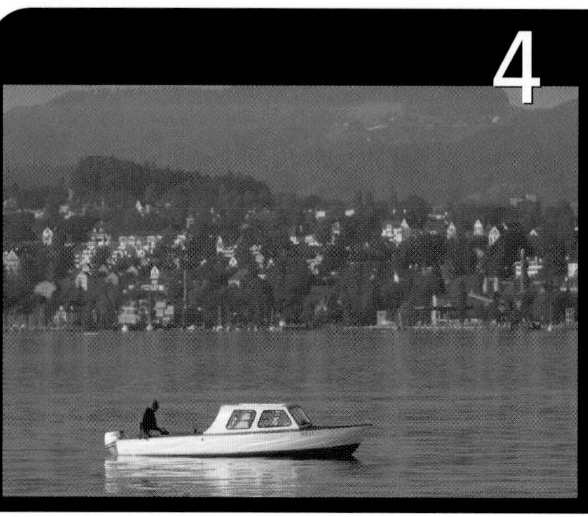

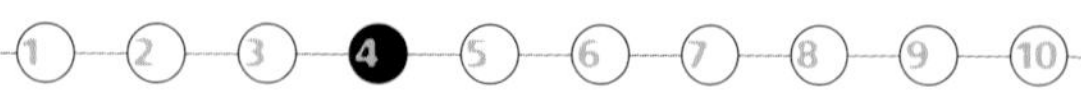

4 Locking a Focus

A camera's autofocus (AF) system works by automatically focusing on the object in the center of the viewfinder. So if you press the shutter-release button while your subject is positioned off-center, your subject will be out of focus, as the camera is automatically set to focus and expose for the object in the center. To focus and expose an off-center subject correctly, you will need to use Focus Lock—a system for telling the camera where to focus.

Using Focus Lock

First, position the subject in the center of your viewfinder. Next, press the shutter-release button halfway to lock the focus at the distance where the subject is. As you press the button, you will hear a click or see the focus indicator (most likely a green dot) light up on the LCD.

After that, reposition the subject so that it is off-center on your LCD. Check that neither you nor your subject move from your original position as you recompose the shot. Finally, press the shutter all the way down to take the picture. By locking the focus first, your subject will be in focus even though it is not centered. As you won't be taking only subject-centered images, practice this technique so that you can compose freely while still keeping your subject in focus.

▲ Press the shutter-release button halfway to lock the focus, and keep your finger in this position.

▲ Photo taken without using Focus Lock.

▲ Position the subject in the center and press the shutter-release button halfway to focus on the subject.

▲ Recompose the shot and press the shutter-release button all the way down to take the photo.

Adjusting Exposure Using Focus Lock

When you lock the focus on a subject, the camera is also set to expose properly for it. In other words, if you lock the focus on a very bright subject, the camera will underexpose the shot in order to expose the subject correctly. The effect of doing this is to make the entire photo appear slightly darker. Conversely, if you lock the focus on a very dark subject, the camera will overexpose the shot and this will make the photo appear slightly brighter.

▲ Underexposing the photo by locking the focus on the brightest area

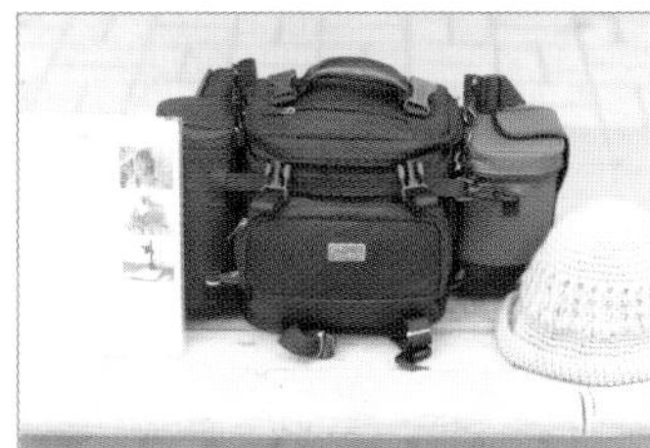

▲ Overexposing the photo by locking the focus on the darkest area

▲ Exposing the picture correctly by locking the focus on a suitable area

▶ Using the Focus Lock function, you can choose which subject to focus on.

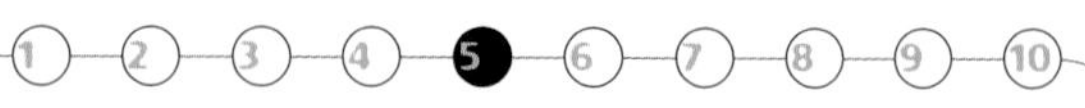

5 Using Lenses

The earliest camera was the pinhole camera, which was just a black box with a pin-sized hole in one of its sides. Pinhole cameras did not use lenses to help them focus light rays, so the images produced were rather blurry. But ever since lenses were incorporated into camera design, things have been very different. Today, there are countless types of lenses that can be built into digital compacts or attached to SLRs.

About the Lens

The term *lens* refers to a transparent substance, usually glass, used in optical devices to change the convergence of light rays. In photography, these pieces are known as lens elements. *Lens* can refer to a single lens element or groups of these elements. Inside a lens, you will also find an iris diaphragm that controls the amount of light entering the camera.

▶▶▶ Aperture

As you have read in the introduction, the aperture is the size of the opening created by the iris diaphragm.

When you open up the aperture, you let in more light. The aperture of a lens is measured on a scale of *f*-stops or *f*-numbers that are fractions of the focal length of the lens. A large aperture would have a small *f*-number, while a small aperture would have a large *f*-number.

Understanding the Terminology of Lenses: An Example

▲ Olympus C-5050 lens

Olympus Super Bright Zoom Lens Olympus uses the term *Super Bright* to describe lenses with a large maximum aperture.

AF Zoom The camera's zoom lens is capable of autofocusing.

_7.1–21.3mm_ These numbers represent the focal length range of the lens. As we learned in the preceding pages, this is equivalent to a focal length range of 35–105mm on a film camera. Note that the maximum focal length of 21.3mm is three times that of the minimum focal length of 7.1mm. So another way of describing the focal length range of a camera like this one is to say that it has a 3X optical zoom.

_1:1.8–2.6_ These numbers indicate the range in aperture size. An aperture size of *f*/1.8 is considered very large for popular digital cameras. For most of us, an aperture of *f*/2.8 or smaller is good enough.

Zooming Effect

If you zoom while using a slow shutter speed, you can create a zooming effect, as shown below. First, set a slow shutter speed. When the shutter is open, zoom into a target while keeping your camera steady.

▲ The zooming effect

 You can achieve the same effect by using the Night Landscape Scene mode, which uses a slow shutter speed.

▶▶▶ Angle of View

The amount of a scene that can be recorded by a lens is called the angle of view. The angle of view depends on the focal length of the lens. A wide-angle lens, as the name suggests, has a wide angle of view, meaning that it can record much of the scene before it. A telephoto lens, on the other hand, has a narrow angle of view and is used for zooming in on subjects at a distance.

In general, lenses with a focal length between 14mm and 50mm (film camera equivalent) are considered wide-angle lenses. Those with focal lengths around 50mm are standard lenses, while lenses longer than 50mm are telephoto lenses. If you have a 3X zoom lens with a focal length of 35mm–105mm, it is comparable to having a wide-angle (35mm) lens, a standard (50mm) lens, and a telephoto (105mm) lens at the same time.

The following photos show the same scene shot with different length lenses. Observe how the focal length affects how small or large the subject appears.

▲ Focal length: 30mm

▲ Focal length: 50mm

▲ Focal length: 100mm

▶▶▶ Perspective

Changing the focal length not only changes how much of the scene you capture, it also changes the perspective. Your subject can seem nearer or farther away from the other subjects depending on the lens you use. When you use a telephoto lens, the perspective is compressed and your subject will appear closer to the background. In contrast, your subject will appear to be farther away from the background if you use a wide-angle lens.

▶▶▶ Depth of Field

Depth of field, also known as depth of focus, is the range of distance in which you can keep the scene sharply focused. When describing depth of field, we say it is either deep or shallow.

In the photo on the right, both the objects and the background are brought into focus so, we say that it has a deep depth of field. In the other photo, the middle object is in focus while everyhing else is blurred, so this photo is said to have a shallow depth of field.

▲ Shallow depth of field

▲ Deep depth of field

Changing the Depth of Field

You can change the depth of field by adjusting the aperture. A large aperture creates a shallow depth of field, while a small aperture creates a deeper depth of field. The results will appear quite different. This is covered in greater detail later in the chapter.

Another way of changing the depth of field is to change the lens. You may have noticed that you get a shallow depth of field when you are close to your subject and a deeper depth of field when you are farther away. In the same way, telephoto lenses (or maximum zoom on your camera), with their long focal length, have a shallow depth of field while wide-angle lenses, with their short focal length, have a deeper depth of field.

In addition, you need to remember that the range of focus in front of and behind a point of focus is unequal. About 1/3 of your depth of field is in front of your point of focus while 2/3 of it is behind.

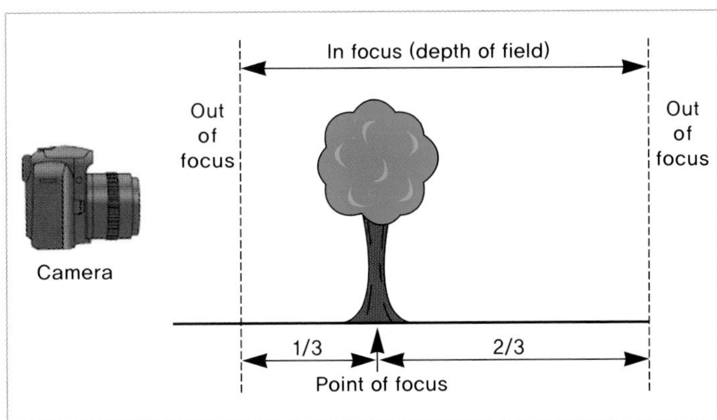

Choosing Between Wide-Angle and Telephoto Lenses

▶▶▶ Wide-Angle Lens (Zoom-Out)

▲ A wide-angle lens is great for shooting scenery.

▶ Shooting objects or buildings with a wide-angle lens exaggerates perspective and makes them look more majestic.

▶ A deep depth of field that allows both the subject and the background to remain in focus

▶▶▶ Telephoto Lens (Zoom-In)

▶ A telephoto lens is a must for taking photos of subjects that you can't approach.

▲ A shallow depth of field gives emphasis to the subject by bringing it into focus against a blurry background.

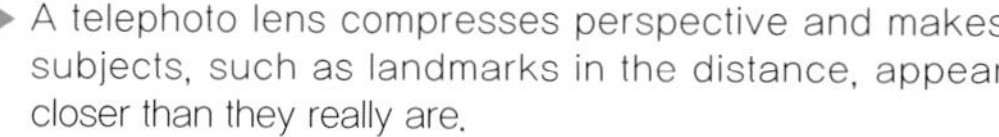

▶ A telephoto lens compresses perspective and makes subjects, such as landmarks in the distance, appear closer than they really are.

▶ It helps to remember that in addition to the background, a telephoto lens will also blur out the foreground elements. In this shot, the cage wires in the foreground are blurred out.

▶ If you don't zoom in enough, the cage wires become more obvious.

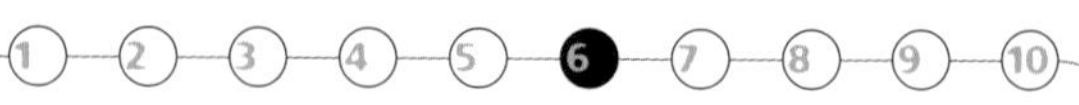

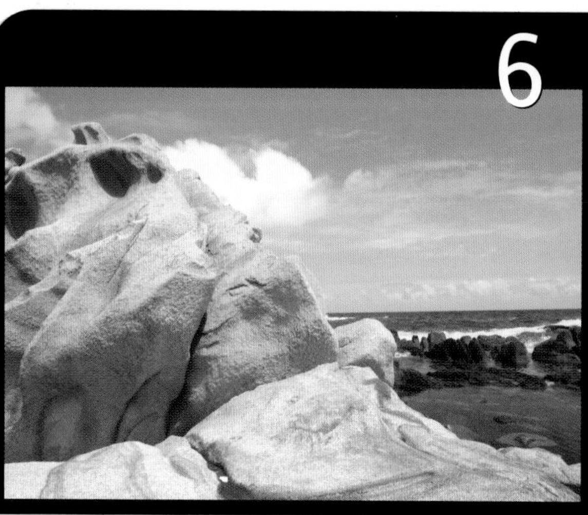

Controlling Exposure

In this section, you will learn to adjust the exposure using automatic cameras with the Exposure Compensation feature and using semiautomatic cameras with the Shutter Priority or Aperture Priority mode. Even if you can't adjust the aperture or shutter speed on your camera, this chapter will help you understand how your camera arrives at the automatic settings and what happens in the Scene modes that are available on most cameras.

What Is Exposure?

Exposure refers to the total amount of light that hits the CCD on a digital camera or the film on a traditional camera. An image is said to be overexposed when the CCD receives too much light and underexposed when it receives too little. Changing the aperture or shutter speed will alter the exposure, but these two methods produce slightly different results.

Adjusting Exposure with Exposure Compensation

Also known as EV (exposure value) adjustment, this feature lets you modify the automatic exposure set by the camera up or down a few levels. A value of 0 represents the exposure suggested by the camera. Select the + values (for example, +0.3, +0.7) to increase the exposure and make the image brighter and the – values (for example, –0.3, –0.7) to decrease the exposure and darken the image.

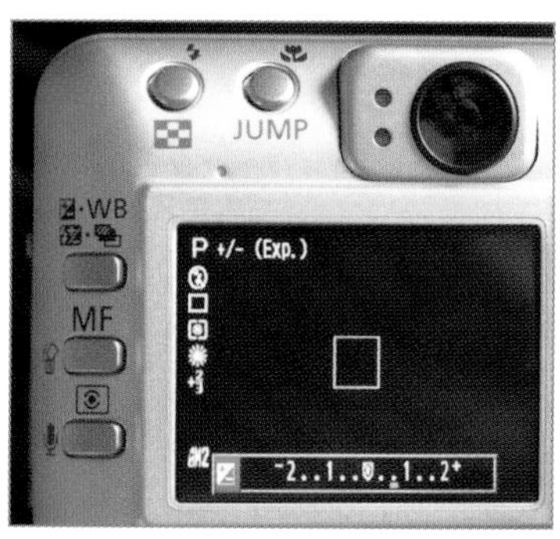

▶ The Exposure Compensation menu

▲ Original exposure at 0

▲ Correct exposure at –0.3

▲ Underexposed at –0.7

Adjusting Exposure with ISO

Another way of adjusting the exposure on a consumer camera is to change the sensitivity of the CCD to light. Check if your camera supports manual ISO adjustment. If it does, increase the ISO when shooting in low-light conditions so that the image needs less light to be properly exposed. If it doesn' t, use additional light sources (candles, flashlight, for example) to brighten up the location. Conversely, use a low ISO, turn off the lights, or provide some shade when shooting in a very bright location.

Adjusting Exposure with Aperture

As you know by now, an aperture is measured on a scale of *f*-stops or *f*-numbers, and the smaller the *f*-number, the bigger the aperture. The stop numbers are *f*/1.0, *f*/1.4, *f*/2, *f*/2.8, *f*/4, *f*/5.6, and so on. The interval between each stop is known as one stop.

The size of the aperture or the amount of light passing through it doubles every time we stop up (use a smaller *f*-number). Conversely, it reduces by half as we stop down (use a larger *f*-number). At an aperture of *f*/4, for example, the amount of light passing through the lens is half of *f*/2.8 but twice as much as *f*/5.6. Lenses with a big maximum aperture are expensive. Most consumer lens apertures may not open wide enough to work well in poorly lit areas.

▲ Underexposed at *f*/5.6: amount of light halved

▲ Correct exposure at *f*/4

▲ Overexposed at *f*/2.8: amount of light doubled

When to Use Aperture Priority Mode

When adjusting exposure in the Aperture Priority mode, you should note that opening up the aperture has the effect of making the depth of field in the image more shallow, causing a loss of detail in the image. The reverse is true when closing the aperture.

▶▶▶ Shallow Depth of Field

To emphasize a subject by bringing it into focus while blurring the background, set the camera to Aperture Priority mode and open up the aperture to create a shallow depth of field. You can get a similar effect by selecting the Portrait mode on an automatic camera.

▲ *f*/1.8 at 1/250 second

▶▶▶ Deep Depth of Field

To make sure that the entire image is sharply focused (especially for scenic shots), use a small aperture to create a deep depth of field. When you use a small aperture, you have to use a slow shutter speed in order to expose the image adequately. The camera automatically adjusts these settings if you select the Landscape mode. A slow shutter speed will make the camera sensitive to movement, so the use of a tripod is recommended.

At times, you can't use a slow shutter speed but you need to have a large depth of field. For instance, you may be taking a shot of people standing at various distances from the camera who can't keep still. In such cases, you can still use a small aperture with a normal shutter speed, but you have to take the shot on a very bright day or environment.

▲ *f*/8 at 1/50 second

Adjusting Exposure with Shutter Speed

The shutter controls the length of time that light enters the camera. A fast shutter speed shortens the exposure time, reducing the total amount of light the CCD receives. On the other hand, a slow shutter speed increases the amount of light entering and is therefore ideal for low-light photography. The range of shutter speeds available is very wide. The more commonly used range is from 2 seconds to 1/500 second. Like aperture intervals, one shutter speed interval is equal to 1 stop. Similarly, a shutter speed of 1 second, for example, is twice as slow as a shutter speed of 1/2 second and lets in double the amount of light.

▲ Correct exposure at a shutter speed of 1/60 second

▲ Overexposed at a shutter speed of 1/30 second: amount of light doubled

▲ Underexposed at a shutter speed of 1/125 second: amount of light halved

▲ Shot at a shutter speed of 1/2 second

▲ Shot at a shutter speed of 1/30 second

▲ Shot at a shutter speed of 1/125 second

When to Use Shutter Priority Mode

Other than its effect on exposure, shutter speed has a tremendous impact on how movement is captured. A fast shutter speed can freeze a subject in motion, which is why you should use fast shutter speeds at sporting events. Using a slow shutter speed captures the motion of moving objects as light trails.

▶▶▶ Fast Shutter Speeds

Set the camera to Shutter Priority mode and use a fast shutter speed to freeze a subject in motion. If you have an automatic camera, you can switch to the Sports mode that automatically sets faster shutter speeds.

As shutter speed increases, more light is needed to properly expose the image, so sunny days and well-lit surroundings, together with high ISO (light sensitivity) settings, are best for such shots.

▶ Shutter speed: 1/8 second

▶▶▶ Slow Shutter Speeds

Try a slow shutter speed to capture the motion streaks of vehicles at night. Remember to use a tripod to prevent camera shake. On an automatic camera, the Night Landscape or Fireworks Show mode produce similar results. While in these modes, the camera uses a slow shutter speed, focuses at infinity, and turns off the flash.

When you use a slow shutter speed, the CCD receives a lot of light, so you should take these shots at night or in dimly lit surroundings to prevent overexposure.

▶ Shutter speed: 30 seconds

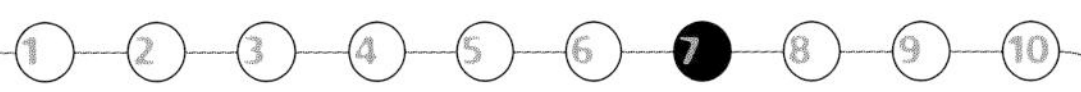

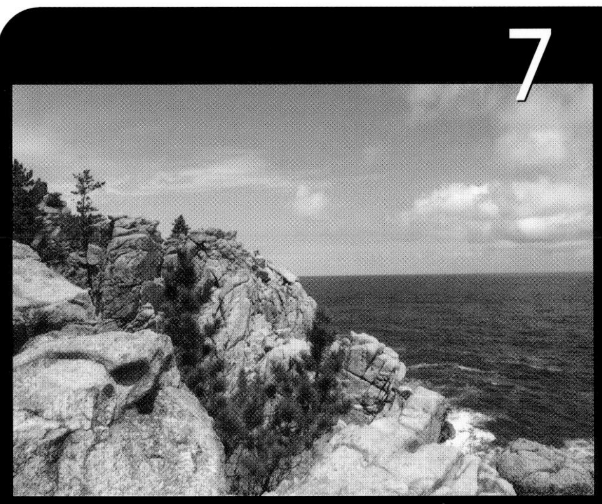

7 Composing a Shot

Composition, in both photography and art, refers to the way in which the elements that make up the work are arranged. While there are clear, technical instructions on how to use a camera, the interpretation of what makes a good composition is subjective. But in spite of the subject's non-specific nature, there are some general guides, and dos and don'ts, that will help you in composing a shot.

Subject Placement

▶▶▶ Place the Subject in the Right Spot

The subject need not be in the center of your photos all of the time. The subject can be in the center, but it can also be off-center for a completely different effect.

tip A well-composed image is one that complements the photographer's vision or ideas. For example, if your aim is to portray your subject in a favorable light, the composition should enhance your subject's characteristics.

▶▶▶ Avoid Interference

A common mistake made by beginners is focusing on getting the subject right but forgetting everything else. Don't fall into that trap. Remember that in order to create a good composition, all elements in the photo must mix well. Before you press the shutter button, check that surrounding objects do not interfere with your main subject. This can take the form of a lamp post or a tree branch sticking out of your subject's head, as shown here.

▲ In the original shot, the railing was interfering with the man, who is the main subject. The photo looks much better when the model moves away from the railing.

▶▶▶ Rule of Thirds

Essentially, the Rule of Thirds is about dividing the frame into thirds horizontally and vertically with two vertical and two horizontal lines. As the rule goes, you will get a pleasing composition if you place your subject along the lines or the intersections of the lines. It is widely acknowledged among photographers that this "rule" is not really a rule; it's more like a guide. In some cases, it may be better to break this rule.

▶ Using the Rule of Thirds in this shot produced a pleasing composition.

tip Before taking a photo, think of how to organize your subjects in order to communicate your theme, and try to visualize the results. While composing an image, most photographers go through the process of repeatedly adding and removing elements before they finally settle on a particular composition. During this process, a photographer has to keep reviewing his vision of the final image. With practice, a photographer will be able to match his vision with reality more closely. Many well-composed shots, especially indoor ones, are not accidental; they were pre-visualized and shot as planned.

▲ You need to develop a "camera's eye" for seeing the world in order to pick out photo opportunities.

▲ The LCD on digital cameras makes it easier to compose a shot.

Horizontal or Vertical?

You can make the same photo look completely different simply by changing the orientation layout, for example horizontal or vertical. The key is in choosing a layout that best highlights the subject's features and characteristics. Horizontal shots, in general, can give a sense of stability to the photo while vertical shots are normally used to shoot tall buildings to give emphasis to height.

▶ A horizontal shot makes the forest look dense and enclosed while a vertical shot includes less of the forest and more of the path and the sky, making the scene look more open and the perspective a little deeper.

▶ The choice between a vertical and horizontal orientation here depends on whether the emphasis is on the chamber pipes or the grand piano.

Filling Up the Frame

A common mistake is to take the shot too far away from the subject. Try moving one step closer to your subject to give it more emphasis vis-à-vis the background. This will help to focus the viewer's attention on the characteristics and features of the subject. This technique will also remove a cluttered or dull background from the photo.

▲ From a long way off, the subject looks insignificant while the background looks featureless. Moving closer captures more of the detail in the subject and the background.

tip Instead of thinking only about adding elements to a scene, you should look at removing unnecessary objects to keep the main point of interest on the subject. You can do this by physically removing the unwanted elements, moving closer, or shooting from a different point of view.

▲ Get closer to get more of the subject and less of the distracting background.

Leading Lines

The environment around us is composed of natural lines—the horizon, winding paths, straight roads, etc. By exploiting the existing lines in a scene, we can move the viewer's gaze across or deeper into the photo, making it a more dynamic and engaging work. These lines—known as leading lines—are often used to direct the point of interest to the main subject.

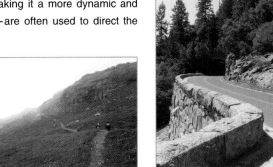

▲ Use leading lines to guide your viewer's gaze into the photo.

Experiment with taking a photo from way above or way below for a fresh point of view that will make your composition stand out from the rest. Even a photo of ordinary subjects can look extraordinary if you shoot it at an interesting angle.

▲ A shot of the other side of the gate taken from the top

▲ A front shot of a gate

Note

We've taken a look at some common compositions, but this does not mean that you should force all of your photos to fit into one of these forms. When composing a shot, it is more important that you evaluate the scene, the mood, and the moment before your eyes and explore compositions that will deliver the theme you have in mind.

In other words, how photos are composed is completely up to you. Instead of restricting your shots to the compositions we discussed in this section, use them as a foundation for creating your own work.

For beginners, we recommend that you practice composing shots using inanimate objects because it will help you to develop a photographer's eye for good subject placement.

▶ Although the the subjects are right in the center and not 1/3 from the edge as spelled out in the Rule of Thirds, the compositions are still pleasing in their simplicity and balance.

Checklist

- Wrap the wrist strap around your wrist and get a good grip on the camera.
- Check that your fingers are not covering the lens or built-in flash.
- Adopt a steady posture, using other objects or a tripod for support if necessary.
- Use Focus Lock to focus on a subject that is not in the center of your viewfinder,
- Adjust the exposure using the Exposure Compensation feature if the image is too dark or too bright.
- Adjust the exposure by changing the aperture or shutter speed if you have a semiautomatic camera.
- Use a large aperture (small *f*-number) to blur the background.
- Use a small aperture (large *f*-number) to keep the entire image focused.
- Use a fast shutter speed to freeze action.
- Use a slow shutter speed to create motion streaks.
- Do not position your subject in the center all of the time.
- Check that surrounding objects do not interfere with your subject.
- Try using the Rule of Thirds.
- Fill up the frame with your subject.
- Look for leading lines in the scene.

40 Digital Photography Techniques

Chapter 2

Exploring More Advanced Features

We have already covered a lot of ground on the technical side of things in the Introduction and Chapter 1. In Chapter 2 we will finish exploring how to use a camera. From Chapter 3 forward, we will look at the techniques for specific themes and situations. But first, let's explore the digital camera's more advanced features.

Some of these features, such as flash, close-ups, and continuous shots, are common to both digital and film cameras, while others, such as Black-and-White and Sepia modes, and white balance, are unique to digital cameras.

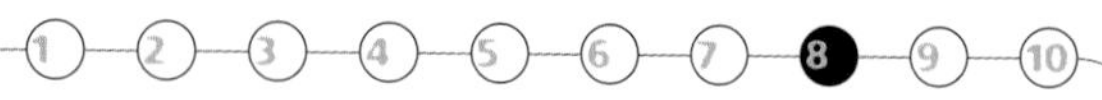

8 Working with Light

The word *photography* means to draw a picture with light, so it goes to show what an important role lighting plays in photography. Since light is such a key element, we will examine in detail the effects of light shining at different angles, at different times of day, and in different weather conditions, and learn to work with each lighting scenario. By the end of this section, you will have learned the essential techniques for working with outdoor light, including light metering methods. We will cover indoor lighting techniques in Technique 20.

A ngle of Light

Avoid taking photos with the light shining directly over a subject, as the harsh lighting will create strong highlights and deep shadows, resulting in a loss of detail. Light thrown at an angle from either side of the subject, or from behind the camera, is often easier to work with. When a subject is lit at an angle, you get a more three-dimensional effect.

▲ A strong light source shining directly over the subject creates harsh shadows. In shots of people, such a light source will deepen dark eye circles.

▲ Diffused light thrown on both sides of the subject lights up the subject's features

Backlighting

Another type of lighting condition to avoid is backlighting, where the light source shines from behind the subject, throwing the subject's features into shadow. As much as you try not to take backlit photos, these shots can't be avoided. For instance, you may need to take a photo of a vacationing friend standing in front of a landmark even though it is backlit.

To make sure that your subject is not left in the shadows, select the Back Light or Fill Flash mode on your camera. The flash will fire automatically to fill in the shadows. If you can adjust the flash's intensity, lower it slightly for a more natural-looking photo.

▲ Backlit photo taken with no flash

▲ Backlit photo taken with Fill Flash

tip A backlit scene is not necessarily a hopeless situation. If the subject is translucent, the light will shine through the subject. The subject will appear luminous and will not be underexposed. If the backlighting is soft and diffused and the background is unimportant, you can set the shutter speed and aperture to expose the subject correctly while overexposing the background. This method, which captures the subject details and foregoes the background image, may work better than using a flash because flash light is usually harsh and unnatural.

▲ As the light shines through the leaves, the veins on the leaves can be seen clearly.

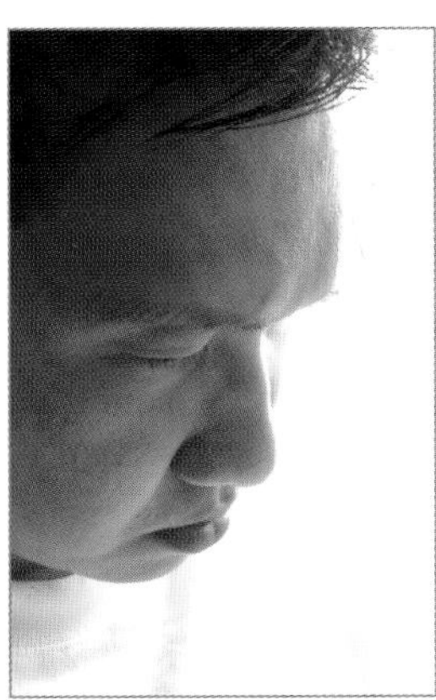

▲ The soft, diffused light from the plane window presented the perfect lighting conditions for a profile shot.

Light-Metering Methods

Light metering is a process of measuring the amount of light reflected off of your subject. Nearly all cameras have a built-in light meter, also known as an exposure meter, which measures light. Depending on whether you are using a manual or automatic camera, the camera will recommend or automatically set the exposure for you. There are three different light-metering methods:

- Matrix Metering: The entire picture in the viewfinder is split into segments that are metered individually. The camera then compares the results to its database of about 100,000 photos and recommends or sets an appropriate exposure.

  This light-metering method is the most suitable for beginners. It is useful for taking snapshots of rapidly moving objects or in situations where fast reaction is needed. On the downside, it will be more difficult to create the effect you want in your photos, as the camera matches the scene before it to a phantom database that you have no control over.

- Center-Weighted Metering: The camera measures the light in the central area of the photo. To use this method, move the camera around the photo area to measure the light reading at different parts. Then decide which part of the photo is most important and set the exposure accordingly.

- Spot Metering: This is the most accurate light-metering method. The camera measures the light at a spot in the center of the photo. Another way to shoot backlit photos is to use spot metering. Switch your camera to Spot Metering mode and point it at the subject. By doing so, you expose the subject correctly while overexposing the background.

tip Since you can't properly expose both foreground and background at the same time due to the wide tonal range in the scene, it makes sense to make sure that your subject's features are not left in the dark even if it means overexposing the background.

▲ Photo taken using matrix metering

▲ Photo taken using spot metering

If you can't meter light using your camera, use the Exposure Compensation menu on your camera to expose a back-lit photo and brighten it up.

Weather

Although many of us assume that photos taken on cloudy days will not turn out well, cloudy days are actually better for taking photos of people and objects. On clear days, you should attempt to take photos of your subject in the shade.

The reason cloudy days and a shady spot on a clear day are better for taking photos is because of the diffused lighting conditions. The clouds act as a filter for the strong sunlight and soften the photo.

However, you should avoid areas in deep shade and refrain from taking photos when the sun is at its brightest. If you must take a photo in the sun, avoid having the sunlight shine directly on your subject.

▲ Strong sunlight is harsh and it also makes your subject squint.

▲ Cloudy days, in general, are better for taking photos of people.

▲ Photo taken at noon (in direct sunlight) on a clear day. The contrast is too strong, making the photo look flat.

▲ On a clear and sunny day, take photos in the shade under a tree, for example, for good results.

Time of Day

Sunrise and sunset photos look very different, as the time of the shoot has an influence on the colors that will appear in your photo. Photos taken before sunrise will have a bluish tint, but photos taken immediately after the sun rises will be reddish. The higher the sun is in the sky, the more accurate and clearer the colors will appear in your photo. This is especially true for shots taken at noon.

As the sun sets, the colors in your photo will appear warmer. Red and orange hues will appear in photos taken in the early evening, but as the sun sets, the sky will be filled with beautiful shades of purple, with hints of pink and green.

These changing colors are why your photo looks different when taken at different times. The colors are warmest and softest approximately one to two hours before sunset. This is the time when most photographers take their photos.

▲ Photo taken at noon

▲ Photo taken in late afternoon

▲ Photo taken during sunset

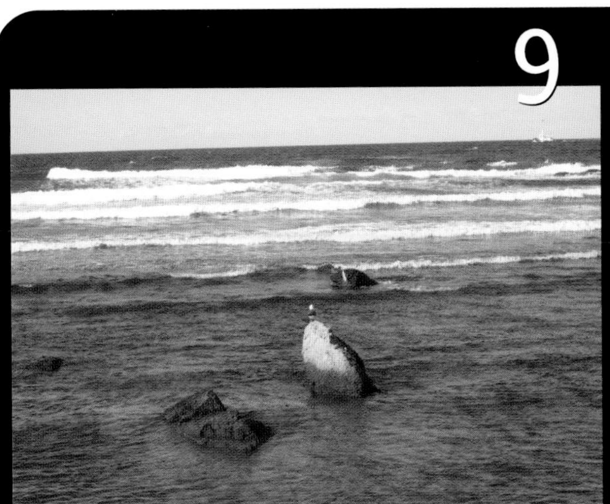

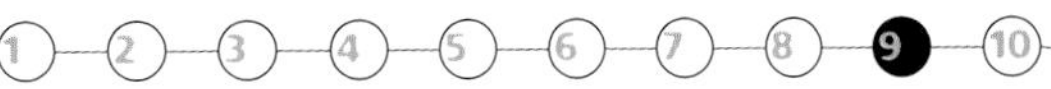

9

Using Flash

The flash, unlike other sources of light that provide continuous lighting, is a sudden burst of bright light. The flash is commonly used to light up backlit subjects, take night photos outdoors, or shoot in poorly lit indoor spaces. A built-in flash can usually light up to a maximum distance of 33 feet (10 meters). This is known as the flash depth. Check your camera specifications for the optimal distance to place your subject from the flash.

Internal Flash

Most digital cameras are equipped with a built-in flash that is either fixed or pops up when triggered. There is no other difference between these two types of built-in flash.

▲ Nikon Coolpix 8700: pop-up flash

▲ Fujifilm Finepix F700: fixed flash

External Flash

High-end cameras have a mount (usually on top) called a hot shoe to which we can attach an external flash. External flash units draw energy from their own battery source, so they have no effect on the battery life of the camera. On better camera models, you can tilt and swivel an attached flash unit to change the direction of light and create different lighting effects.

▲ Hot shoe

As most digital cameras do not have a hot shoe, we use a bracket to attach an external flash.

▶ Use a bracket on cameras without a hot shoe to attach an external flash.

Flash Modes

There are four basic Flash modes: Auto, Anytime (Fill Flash), Flash Cancel (Off), and Red-Eye Reduction. Depending on the model, some cameras also come with Slow Sync and Daylight Sync modes. Check your user manual to see which Flash modes your camera supports before continuing.

▶▶▶ Auto Mode

As the name suggests, the camera checks the intensity of the light in the surrounding area and automatically pops the flash if the lighting is poor. In most cases, you would use the Auto mode to take pictures. This mode is great for beginners because you can take pictures without having to think about lighting (the camera does the thinking for you), but this mode tends to light up your subject and leave the background in darkness.

▲ The background in this Auto Flash shot did not turn out dark because the model was positioned near the wall, which reflected the light from the flash.

▶▶▶ Anytime Flash (Fill Flash) Mode

In this mode, the flash is set to go off whenever a photo is taken.

▶▶▶ Flash Cancel (Off) Mode

In this mode, the flash will not fire even when the lighting is poor. This mode is used when you want to take certain types of photos (silhouette, for example) or when taking photos at close range. If you fire the flash when you are very near your subject, the image will be overexposed.

▶▶▶ Red-Eye Reduction Mode

In poorly lit areas, our pupils will dilate to take in more light. So, when the flash is fired in low-light areas, the light from the flash will enter the dilated pupils and bounce off the blood vessels at the back of the eyes, creating the red-eye syndrome we see in many photographs. In Red-Eye Reduction mode, a small, preliminary flash goes off to give the eyes time to adjust to brighter light so that the pupils will constrict by the time the second flash is fired.

▲ Red eyes seen in a photo taken using the Auto mode

▲ Using the Red–Eye Reduction mode to prevent the red–eye syndrome

Eliminating Red Eyes

A way to work around the red-eye problem is to take a profile shot of your subject so that her eyes are not staring directly into the camera. But the best way, of course, is to increase the ambient lighting so that your subject's pupils won't expand as much.

▶▶▶ Slow Sync Mode or Night Flash

If you use the Auto mode to take a portrait shot at night, the subject gets most of the flash while the background remains dark. To prevent this from happening, use the Slow Sync mode. This activates the flash at the start of the exposure time and engages a slow shutter speed to let in more light and keep both subject and background illuminated.

On the flip side, however, you have to use a tripod, as even the slightest camera movement will blur your image as a result of the slow shutter speed. If you have a tripod and the time to set up the shot, this mode is recommended.

▲ Auto mode: creates high-contrast images with harsh shadows.

▲ Slow Sync mode: captures more ambient light and creates better tonal range.

▶▶▶ Daylight Sync Mode

In this mode, the flash is set to fire even during the day to obtain an appropriate exposure. This mode is especially useful for taking more natural shots of backlit subjects. For example, let's say you are taking a photo of a subject who is standing in front of a window in daytime. The background is sufficiently bright, but shadows fall on your subject's face. Under such circumstances we would use the flash to illuminate both the subject and the background equally.

Softening the Flash

As the flash is a momentary burst of bright light, it is great for taking a freeze frame of moving subjects and for avoiding the motion blur caused by unsteady hands. When used under normal conditions, however, a strong flash can create harsh shadows and may produce washed-out photos. You can overcome this problem by lowering the flash output using the following accessories:

▶▶▶ Diffuser

If you have an external flash unit, attach a diffuser to lower the flash output and soften the light. Compare the photos on the right. You can see that the shot taken without a diffuser has harsh shadows while the other looks softer and has captured more of the detail on the wall.

▲ Shot without a diffuser

▲ Shot with a diffuser

Although you cannot attach a diffuser to an internal flash, you can use semiopaque adhesive tape, plain white paper, or some other common everyday object to cover the flash and act as a diffuser.

▲ An inexpensive way of diffusing the light from a built-in flash

▶▶▶ Omni-Bounce

If you have an external flash, you can buy a semiopaque white cover called an omni-bounce to act as a diffuser.

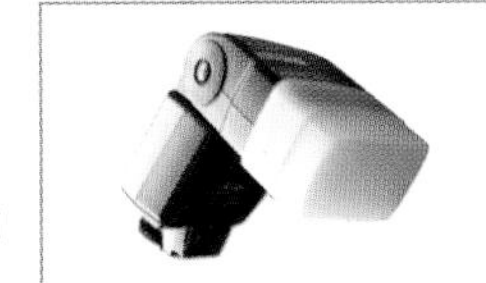

▶ An external flash fitted with an omni-bounce.

▶▶▶ Reflector

You can either buy a reflector or make one yourself. Any large piece of white board can be used as a reflector. By bouncing the flash off the reflector, you can diffuse the light and fill in the shadows.

Alternatively, you can use a nearby wall or a low ceiling as a reflector if you have an external flash. Whatever you use, pick something white so that there won't be an unwanted color cast over your picture.

If you are using a reflector, there is no need to use the Slow Sync Flash mode. Most cameras are set to a flash speed of 1/60 second, which is fast enough for shooting without a tripod. All you need to do is set up the shot and take the photo.

▲ To avoid under- or overexposing a photo, take a trial shot to estimate the flash intensity and exposure required.

▲ Use the Exposure Compensation feature on the camera to get the right exposure.

▲ Comparing an image taken under direct flash (left) and one with flash bounced off the ceiling (right)

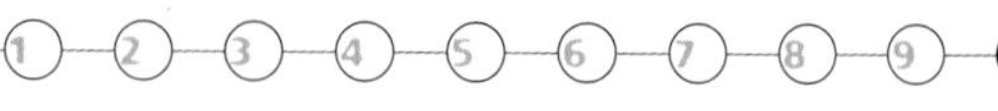

10 Creating Black-and-White and Sepia Images

Before color film was sold commercially in the 1930s, most photographs were in monochrome. These monochrome photographs were normally in black and white or toned to a certain color such as sepia. In photography, B&W is the popular abbreviation for black and white. In this section, we will look at the subjects and themes that are great for B&W and sepia photography.

About Black-and-White and Sepia Modes

With traditional film cameras, you have to use black-and-white film if you want to take black-and-white photos or soak a black-and-white photograph in a toning solution if you want to produce sepia images. With a digital camera, you'll only need to switch to the Black-and-White or Sepia modes.

▲ Turn the camera mode dial to the Image Adjustment mode.

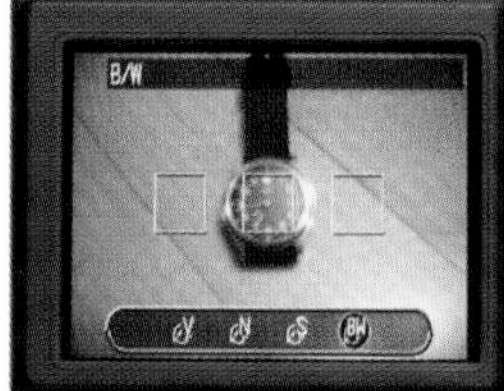

▲ Black–and–White

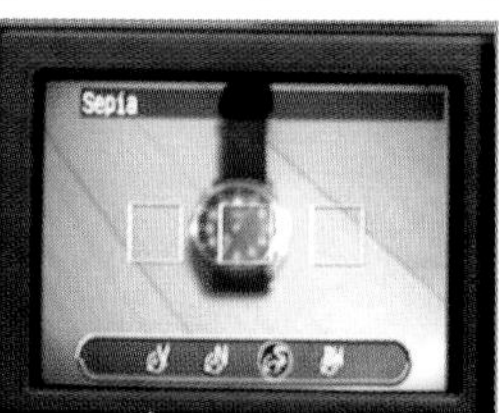

▲ Sepia

Subjects and Themes

Photographers sometimes shoot in black and white or sepia to create a certain style or mood or to fix problems that will show up in color photos. Let's have a look at some of the situations where you may want to consider shooting in black and white.

▶▶▶ Photojournalistic Style

Photojournalistic style is a form of journalism that uses pictures as the primary medium to tell a story. This journalistic style, which uses only supplementary text, is most frequently seen in newspapers or current affairs magazines.

▲ Capturing this scene of a demolition site in black and white makes the scene look like a war photo.

▶▶▶ Antiquated Objects or Buildings

Antiquated objects, historical buildings, or old streets make great subjects for shooting in the Sepia or Black-and-White modes.

▲ You can make a recent shot look old by shooting in the Sepia mode.

▲ You can also take a shot in black and white to convey a sense of history.

▶▶▶ Simplification

With color photos, the presence of different colors and different shades of colors can be very distracting. When there is color in an image, you have to consider how the colors interact. For example, you will have to think about whether the colors contrast (for example, red and green) or form a continuous blend (for example, yellow and orange).

▲ After color is removed from the image, the texture on the rose petals becomes more obvious.

When you can't get the colors to look right in an image, you can consider shooting in black and white or sepia. This will remove the colors from the image, creating a simpler composition. With black-and-white or sepia images, the focus is on the shape, form, or lines and the tonal range in the image. Tonal range refers to the range of brightness or darkness in the image. A high-contrast image will have a wide tonal range while a low-contrast image will have a narrow tonal range.

▲ Taking this shot in Sepia mode makes the leaves that interfere with the chair less distracting and keeps the focus on the chair.

▲ Take black-and-white images of objects with strong outlines for an abstract study of shape and form.

▶▶▶ People Photography

Taking sepia or black-and-white pictures of people or events can give the images a timeless quality. The sepia and black-and-white photography styles are especially popular with weddings and portraits.

▲ You can create a photo journal for weddings.

▲ Sepia and black-and-white images of people can create a feeling of nostalgia.

▲ High-contrast black-and-white or sepia images of people and landscape can look very dramatic.

▶▶▶ Others

There are two other less common situations for taking black-and-white images. First, if you need to take photos of documents or text, it is better to take the shot in black and white, as the high contrast makes the words easier to read. Second, you should note that black-and-white images take up less memory space, so if you do not have much memory left in your camera, you can consider taking black-and-white images.

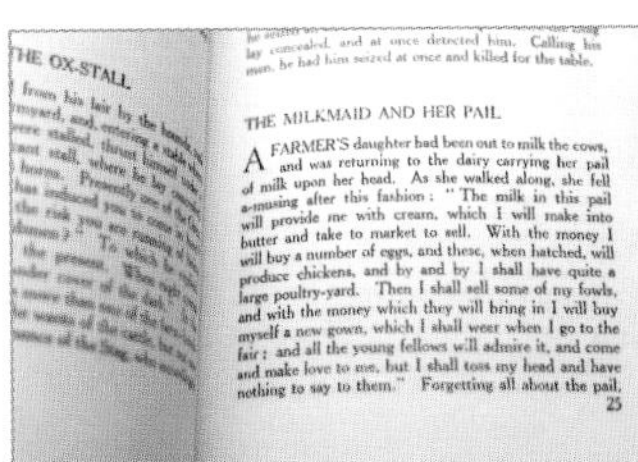

THE OX-STALL

lay concealed, and at once detected him. Calling his men, he had him seized at once and killed for the table.

THE MILKMAID AND HER PAIL

A FARMER'S daughter had been out to milk the cows, and was returning to the dairy carrying her pail of milk upon her head. As she walked along, she fell a-musing after this fashion: "The milk in this pail will provide me with cream, which I will make into butter and take to market to sell. With the money I will buy a number of eggs, and these, when hatched, will produce chickens, and by and by I shall have quite a large poultry-yard. Then I shall sell some of my fowls, and with the money which they will bring in I will buy myself a new gown, which I shall wear when I go to the fair; and all the young fellows will admire it, and come and make love to me, but I shall toss my head and have nothing to say to them." Forgetting all about the pail,

25

▲ The words in an image become easier to read if the image is in black and white.

▲ The image size of this color photograph is 272KB.

▲ The image size of the same photograph in black-and-white is 149KB.

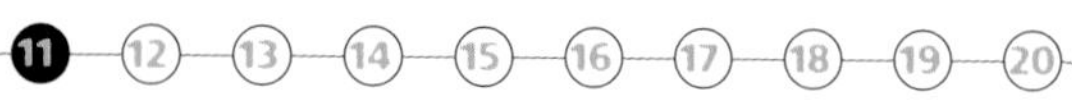

Shooting Close-Ups of Small Objects

Another term for taking close-ups of small objects is *macro photography*. Macro photography can open up a whole new world by revealing amazing details of the things around you. Some possible objects for close-up shots are flowers, insects, and water droplets. With a traditional film camera, you need to buy a macro lens designed for taking close-up shots. With a digital camera, you can save all that money, as the Macro mode is found on most digital cameras.

Definition

Strictly speaking, macro photography means that the subject is reproduced at a magnification of 1:1 or greater on the image. For example, if a petal is 1cm long, its image will be 1cm or larger. Macro photography is also used loosely to mean close-up photography.

Technical Requirements

▶▶▶ Focus

• Focal Length

The minimum focusing distance (focal length) of the lens determines how close you can get to the object. In order to get a good close-up, the focal length should ideally be 10cm or less. Cameras with a good macro feature will allow you to get within 2cm of the object. As the macro feature differs between cameras, you need to look up your camera's specifications in your user's manual.

tip Focal Length of Digital Cameras

Most digital cameras have lenses with a shorter focal length than those in traditional film cameras, making them better at shooting close-ups.

Focal Range

When shooting close-ups, the depth of field in your photos can drop greatly. This means that you have to work with a small focal range. For example, if you are taking a close-up of the dial pad on your cell phone, only some of the numbers on the dial pad will be in focus. Now, this is fine if this is the effect that you are looking for, but it will be a problem if it is not. Therefore, when using the Macro mode, you need to pay attention to the range where the object is in focus. You can, however, increase the focal range by closing up the aperture.

▲ Notice how this close-up looks less sharp toward the edges.

▲ Closing up the aperture increases the focal range and brings the edges back into focus.

▶▶▶ Lighting

Lighting conditions have a great impact on close-up shots taken indoors. Poor lighting conditions will make it difficult to focus on the object and your images will be underexposed. A single fluorescent lamp, for example, cannot light up a room sufficiently for a photo shoot.

Built-In Flash

Using a digital camera's built-in flash for close-ups will overexpose the images, resulting in a loss of detail. You should use an external light source instead to get the right exposure and keep the detail in your photos.

External Light Source

The most accessible type of external light source is a desk lamp. However, the regular incandescent (tungsten, for example) bulbs in these lamps will give a warm orange tone to your photos. In order to capture the natural color of your objects, use an inverter lamp, which emits light similar to daylight.

tip Intensity

When using an external light source, remember that brighter does not always mean better. You should adjust the light's intensity to enhance the object's texture and the mood of the photo. If necessary, use more than one lamp to get the desired effect.

● Angle

You must also consider the angle of the lighting. If the object is made of a reflective material, adjust the angle of the light so that the reflection is not apparent in the photo. Generally speaking, lighting the object from the side will highlight its texture and details.

▶▶▶ Background

A busy background detracts the focus from the main object. So, when shooting close-ups, you want to simplify the background as much as possible. One of the techniques is to use a background sheet. If the object is brightly colored, use a dark background sheet, but if the object is dark, use a light or brightly colored background sheet.

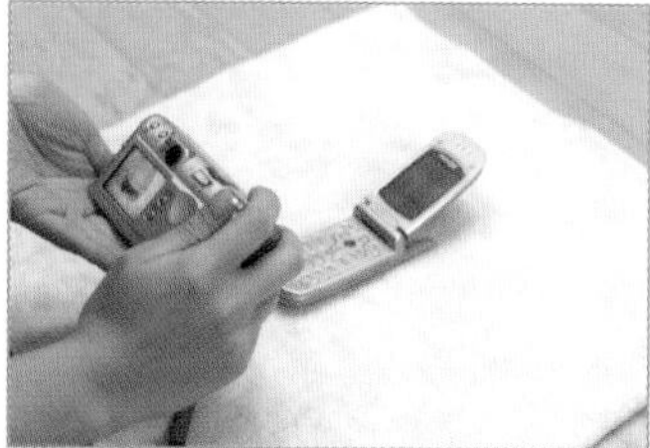

▲ Use a background sheet to simplify the background.

▲ Use dark background sheets for bright and colorful objects.

▲ Use a light background sheet for darker objects.

▶▶▶ Exposure

Taking an exposure reading on a small object can be tricky. You could end up with a reading of the background instead. To avoid this problem, use the more accurate Spot Metering mode when shooting close-ups.

▶▶▶ Using a Tripod

While shooting close-ups, the slightest movement or camera shake will give you a blurred photo. Therefore, you should always use a tripod whenever possible. A tabletop tripod is very useful for shooting close-up photos indoors.

Choosing a Theme

You have many options when it comes to choosing a subject for close-ups. You can take close-ups of flowers, insects, jewelry, or even documents and pictures for your journal. In this section, we will look at some techniques for shooting some popular subjects for close-ups.

▲ A black background is used to keep the point of interest on the subject.

▶▶▶ Flowers

Flowers are a popular choice with most novice photographers. The main concern here is the wind factor. It can be hard to keep flowers or other objects that move in the wind in focus. If a flower doesn't stop swaying, use your hand or another object to hold it in place.

▲ Capturing the vivid colors of a flower using the Macro mode

▶▶▶ Insects

Taking close-ups of insects is more difficult as they are usually small and mobile, making them challenging subjects. If you approach an insect slowly and quietly, you may be able to get a quick shot before it gets away.

An alternative method is to place your camera on a tripod and set it to focus on a spot likely to attract insects, such as a flower, for instance. Wait at a distance away from the camera. When the insect moves into place, use the camera's remote control to take the shot. You can take multiple shots with this setup and later choose the best photo from the lot.

You need good observation skills and some practice in order to take good close-ups of fast-moving insects. For beginners, it is best to start with slower insects first.

▲ Taking photos of ants requires super macro focal lengths of 5cm or less.

▲ Taking photos of butterflies or other insects requires patience and practice.

Documents

You can photograph documents of up to A4 in size if you are using a digital camera with a high resolution. This feature is useful, for instance, when you find a good passage in a book and you need to make a copy for your own notes. But before you photograph any documents, do take note of any restrictions and laws, and be wary of infringing upon any rights.

For good results, you should always use a tripod and illuminate the documents with an external light source. Dim surroundings will underexpose the photos and make the images fuzzy. Additionally, check that the page is properly secured and place the camera vertically over the page. You can photograph several pages at once or, if you want better-quality images, shoot a page in sections.

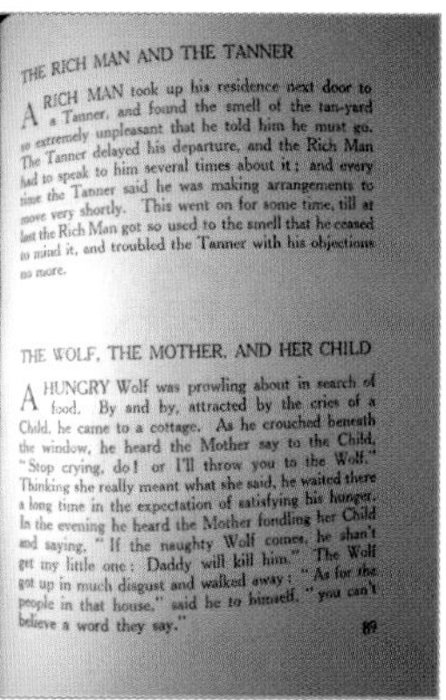

THE RICH MAN AND THE TANNER

A RICH MAN took up his residence next door to a Tanner, and found the smell of the tan-yard so extremely unpleasant that he told him he must go. The Tanner delayed his departure, and the Rich Man had to speak to him several times about it; and every time the Tanner said he was making arrangements to move very shortly. This went on for some time, till at last the Rich Man got so used to the smell that he ceased to mind it, and troubled the Tanner with his objections no more.

THE WOLF, THE MOTHER, AND HER CHILD

A HUNGRY Wolf was prowling about in search of food. By and by, attracted by the cries of a Child, he came to a cottage. As he crouched beneath the window, he heard the Mother say to the Child, "Stop crying, do! or I'll throw you to the Wolf." Thinking she really meant what she said, he waited there a long time in the expectation of satisfying his hunger. In the evening he heard the Mother fondling her Child and saying, "If the naughty Wolf comes, he shan't get my little one: Daddy will kill him." The Wolf got up in much disgust and walked away: "As for the people in that house," said he to himself, "you can't believe a word they say."

89

▲ Photos of documents

Barrel Distortion

When you take a close-up of a shape with distinct outlines (documents, for example), you will sometimes see it bending or rounding at the edges in the photo. This phenomenon is known as barrel distortion and is a necessary artifact of a camera's zoom lens.

Many photos taken with digital and compact film cameras that have zoom capabilities suffer from barrel distortion. For example, with a 35–105mm zoom lens, barrel distortion is most pronounced when the lens is set at 35mm. To reduce barrel distortion, you should set the lens at 70mm or somewhere in the middle of the zoom range, or set the camera to Macro mode when you want to take close-ups of small objects.

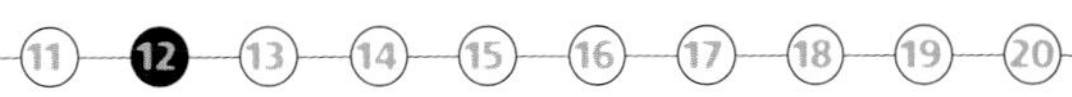

Taking Continuous Shots

Many digital and film cameras have a Continuous Shot function, which allows you to take several photos in succession every second or so. Because you do not have to worry about wasting film in digital cameras, you can use this feature more often than you would with a film camera.

Understanding the Continuous Shot Feature

To shoot continuous photos, switch to the Continuous Shot mode and hold down the shutter-release button. After the shots are taken, the camera will take some time to record all the shots. During this time, the camera is in limbo and you cannot use it to take another shot. There are three factors to consider when evaluating or comparing the Continuous Shot function:

▶▶▶ Frames Per Second (FPS)

This is the number of photos that can be taken every second. Most digital cameras can take 2 or 3 photos per second, but high-end ones can take 10 to 15 per second.

▶▶▶ Maximum Number of Continuous Shots

This is the maximum number of continuous shots the camera can take while the shutter button is pressed. "A maximum of 15 shots recorded at 3 fps," for example, means that the camera can take continuous shots for up to 5 seconds at the rate of 3 frames per second.

▶▶▶ Speed and Quality of Continuous Shots

Image resolution and quality are inversely related to the number of consecutive pictures that can be taken. For example, lowering the image resolution of a camera that takes a maximum of 15 pictures at 2 fps could increase the maximum number of pictures to 20 and improve the speed to 3 fps. Conversely, increasing the image resolution will result in fewer pictures taken and a slower fps rate. Check your user manual for your Continuous Shot function's speed and quality. It will read something like "2 fps at maximum resolution."

▲ Fujifilm Finepix S7000 Zoom (5 fps)

When to Use Continuous Shots

▶▶▶ Fast-Moving Subjects

The trouble with shooting fast-moving subjects is in capturing them at the right moment. With the Continuous Shot feature, you can take successive shots of a single scene very quickly, select the ones you like best, and delete the rest. This increases your chances of getting a well-composed image of such fast-moving objects or people as a train roaring past, a bird in flight, or your child running in the school race.

▲ Subjects moving randomly are hard to compose and keep in focus.

▲ Choose the best photo from the selection.

▶▶▶ Action Sequences

This feature is also useful for capturing the full sequence of a subject's motion. You may, for instance, want to record the fleeting expressions of your baby or give a blow-by-blow account of a sports event in photos. You could also ask a friend to take continuous shots of your golf swing so you can review and correct your posture.

▲ Using the Continuous Shot feature to capture the train at the right distance

Using the Continuous Shot Feature

▶▶▶ Lighting

Typically, the built-in flash is disabled during the Continuous Shot mode. If it is not, you should turn it off. This is because the flash cannot keep up with the speed of the continuous shots, so it will only be activated for the initial shot, leaving the rest underexposed.

With no flash, you have to make sure that the scene is sufficiently lit before shooting. If you are shooting indoors, use an external light source to improve the lighting conditions. If possible, you should also set the camera to a high ISO value for greater light sensitivity.

▲ The flash was activated in only the first of the four continuous shots.

▶▶▶ Shutter Speed

In most cameras, the shutter speed is automatically set to 1/30 second or faster to prevent motion blur. If you can adjust the shutter speed, set it to a minimum of 1/100 second when shooting fast-moving subjects.

▶▶▶ Auto Focus (AF) Mode

If you take continuous shots in the AF mode, the camera needs time to auto focus each shot and this can lower the speed at which your camera takes consecutive photos. If you know the direction your subject is traveling, pre-focus at a point in the frame and press the shutter when your subject comes into frame.

Other Types of Continuous Shots

Other than the Continuous Shot feature, some digital cameras have other modes—such as Auto Exposure Bracketing, Best Shot Selector, Interval mode—that take continuous shots. These shots are different from those taken in the Continuous Shot mode in terms of quality, exposure, interval, or size as they are meant to be used differently.

▶▶▶ Auto Exposure Bracketing (AEB)

The camera will shoot at three different exposures in three continuous shots when you use AEB, or Auto Exposure Bracketing. For example, if the AEB is set to 1 stop, the camera will take the first shot at its recommended exposure, underexpose the second shot by 1 stop, and overexpose the third by 1 stop.

The AEB feature is good for situations where the light condition changes constantly, or when it is difficult to determine the exposure through the LCD.

▲ Recommended exposure

▲ 1 stop underexposure

▲ 1 stop overexposure

tip The AEB function, which is found in most digital cameras, sets the white balance, light sensitivity, and exposure automatically.

▶▶▶ Best Shot Selector

In the Continuous Shot mode, the camera will take consecutive shots up to the maximum number of shots supported by the camera as long as the shutter button is pressed down. If you use the Best Shot Selector, the camera will only save three or four of the sharper and better images to the memory card. This feature is recommended when you have difficulty getting the correct exposure and white balance for stationary subjects.

▶▶▶ Interval Mode

When using the Interval mode, you need to set the shutter-release interval. When the shutter-release button is pressed, the camera will take continuous shots according to the interval setting. The interval range can be between a few seconds to a few minutes. For best results, you should use a tripod.

Unlike the Continuous Shot mode, the Interval mode can only be found in high-end digital cameras. This mode is great for capturing the action sequence of slow-moving subjects like a snail moving along or a flower beginning to bloom. The feature is not designed for capturing fast-moving subjects.

▶▶▶ Nikon's Multi-Shot 16 Feature

Nikon's digital cameras are programmed with a Continuous Shot feature called the Multi-Shot 16. In this mode, you shoot 16 consecutive thumbnail pictures by pressing the shutter button just once. Instead of saving them as separate, individual images, these thumbnails are combined on a single image like a collage.

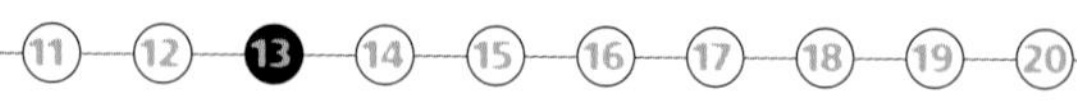

13 Taking Action Shots

In this section, you will learn to capture a freeze frame of a moving subject. For beginners, the challenge is twofold. In terms of equipment, you will need at least a semiautomatic camera to consistently succeed at keeping a moving subject sharp in action shots. With automatic cameras, it is often a hit-or-miss affair. Action shots are also challenging technically, but you will learn all of the techniques in this section.

Stance

It is always important that you keep still while taking a shot, and this is even more so when you are shooting a moving subject, as the slightest movement will result in a blurred image. Adopt the positions we looked at in Technique 2, "Preventing Camera Shake and Blurring" or use a tripod.

Shutter Speed

For most moving subjects, you need to use a shutter speed of 1/250 second or faster. The shutter speed can be set using the Shutter Priority or Manual modes. Alternatively, you can set a large aperture using the Aperture Priority mode to force the camera to use a fast shutter speed to prevent overexposure. An aperture of *f*/2.8 or wider (i.e., smaller *f*-number) is usually large enough. With an automatic camera, you should switch to the Sports Scene mode ( ). You are more likely to take good action shots with the Sports Scene mode if the shot is taken in bright surroundings. The brightness will force the camera to use a faster shutter speed.

▲ To capture the right moment in sports photography, you need to keep your eyes behind the camera for the duration of the event. This shot is taken using a shutter speed of 1/250 second.

Sensitivity

If you can't get a fast enough shutter speed, you can try raising the camera's sensitivity to light so that the camera needs less light to be properly exposed, and you can use a faster shutter speed. Because increasing the sensitivity introduces noise into your picture, this method should only be used as a last resort.

Panning and Tilting

To create a sense of movement in a picture, you can set a slow shutter speed and then move the camera using your hand or a tripod as a pivot to follow the subject's movement as you shoot. This will keep the subject in focus while blurring the background along the movement of your camera.

Moving the camera along the horizontal axis is called panning while tilting moves the camera vertically. The key to keeping a moving subject sharp while blurring the background is to follow the subject at the same pace that it is moving.

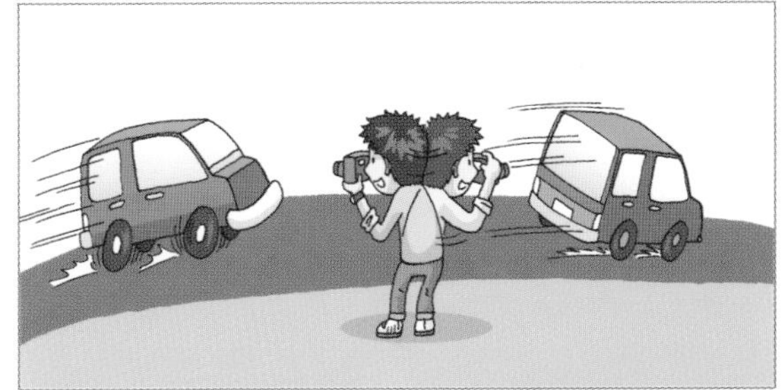

▲ Panning gives an image the sensation of movement.

▲ Tilting is used to take a picture of kids on a seesaw.

▲ Using both panning and tilting together.

When panning or tilting, you can adjust the amount of blur in the background by changing the focal length of the lens and the shutter speed. The amount of blur is also dependent on the subject's speed, the distance between the camera and the subject, and the distance between the subject and the background. The more blurry the background, the faster the subject will be seen as moving.

▶▶▶ Focal Length

To create a more blurry background, you can use a telephoto lens or zoom in to fill your frame with the subject. When the view is magnified, moving the camera will blur the background even more. Conversely, zooming out will make the subject smaller in the frame and create a background with less blur.

▶▶▶ Shutter Speed

Another way of creating a more blurry background is to use a slow shutter speed while moving the camera. With slow shutter speeds, the subject would have moved a fair distance during the shutter release. This will allow you to pan more and create more blur in the background. With faster shutter speeds, the object wouldn't have moved much so the background will not be as blurred. When using slow shutter speeds, you want to be able to keep up with the subject. If you are unable to follow the subject with the camera, the subject will end up looking blurred too.
For motor vehicles on the road, a shutter speed of 1/60 second is usually long enough to blur out the background. To photograph a person walking, a shutter speed of 1/30 second (or greater, if you are able to keep up with the person without causing camera shake) is adequate.

▶▶▶ Object Speed

A fast-moving object lets you move the camera quickly, and this in turns create more blur in the background.

▶▶▶ Distance

The distance between the subject and the background is another factor to consider. The greater this distance, the less blurry will be the background in the picture. Let's think about this for a minute. Say your camera is following the movement of a car and the background is a mountain in a distance. In this case, since the mountain is so far away, the relative position of the mountain hardly changes during the shutter release, resulting in less blur in the background. On the other hand, if you're taking a picture of a car whizzing through the city streets, the buildings in the background will show up in the picture as a complete blur.

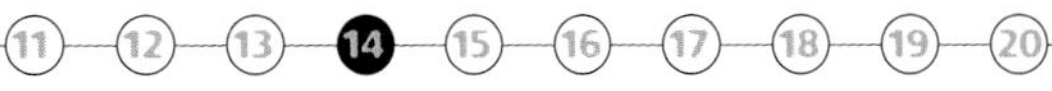

14 Using White Balance

When professional photographers assess the lighting conditions of a location, the intensity of the light source is not the only factor they consider. This is because a shot of two equally lit scenes can look quite different with one looking warmer and the other, cooler. This has to do with the color temperature of the light source. By using the White Balance feature on your digital camera, you can offset the color casts created by a light source's color temperature.

Properties of Light

▶▶▶ Natural and Artificial Light

Light from the sun is natural light. Examples of artificial light sources are incandescent light, fluorescent light, and flash from the camera. Light from the sun or from a light bulb may appear white or colorless to you. However, if you pass the light through a prism, you can see that it actually contains a range of colors as in a rainbow. Light from different sources contains a mixture of these colors in varying proportions, with each light source having its own distinct color.

▶▶▶ Color Temperature

The color of a light source is best described by its color temperature, which is calibrated in degrees Kelvin (°K). Color temperature is a term borrowed from physics and is used to measure the quality of a light source. As the color temperature gets higher, the color moves from red toward blue.

In photography, the term daylight is used to describe the color temperature of sunlight between 10 a.m. and 2 p.m., which is about 5500°K. The color temperature of a tungsten light bulb is about 3000°K. Therefore, we say that daylight is much bluer than the light from a tungsten bulb, which has a reddish tint.

What Is White Balance?

Our eyes automatically adjust to different color temperatures so that a white piece of paper always looks white whether we view it by sunlight or incandescent light. Unlike the human eye, the image sensor in digital cameras records the color temperature of a light source, and this will appear in the photo as a color cast.

For example, if a scene is illuminated by a tungsten light bulb, the image will have an orange cast. The image sensor, therefore, has to be adjusted according to the color temperature of the light source in order to reproduce the colors in the scene accurately.

You can make this adjustment using the White Balance feature, which records the current lighting conditions or color temperature. The camera then adjusts the sensor's relative sensitivity to the colors so that the whites in the scene will also appear white in the image.

White Balance Modes

White is most accurately reproduced on clear days, which is why photos taken in sunlight preserve the natural color of objects. Under other lighting conditions, you need to select one of the White Balance modes for accurate results. Before you shoot, earmark a white piece of paper, area, or object in the scene as a reference point.

Next, select a White Balance mode and preview the results on the LCD monitor. Try a few modes until you get the result you want. Here's what the different modes are for:

▶▶▶ Auto

Adjusts the white balance automatically for lights with a color temperature between 4200°K and 7000°K. If the color temperature falls outside this range, the colors in the captured image may differ from the actual colors.

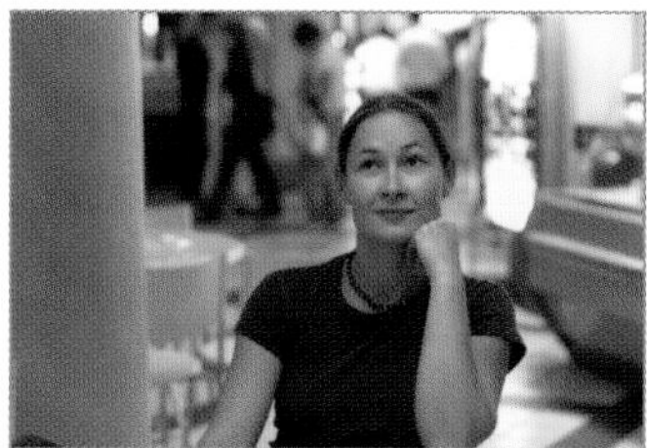

▲ Auto White Balance

▶▶▶ Incandescent

Corrects the color of objects shot under incandescent lights. Color temperature is fixed at approximately 3000°K.

▲ Tungsten White Balance mode

▶▶▶ Fluorescent

Corrects the color of objects shot under fluorescent lights. Color temperature is fixed at approximately 4500°K.

▲ Fluorescent White Balance mode

▶▶▶ Fine

This setting is programmed for taking pictures in direct sunlight on a clear day. Color temperature is fixed at approximately 6000°K. When taking photos outdoors on a clear day, both the Auto and Fine White Balance modes will preserve the natural skin tone.

▲ Daylight White Balance mode

▶▶▶ Cloudy

Programmed for shooting pictures under an overcast sky. Color temperature is fixed at approximately 7000–8000°K.

▲ Flash White Balance mode

Chapter 2

▶▶▶ Custom

Enables you to adjust the white balance manually to match the lighting conditions. If the weather is bad, or if you are taking photos indoors or under colored lights, the best way to reproduce accurate colors is to preset the Custom White Balance mode using a white piece of paper or any white objects.

▲ Custom White Balance mode helps to maintain the natural skin tone.

Setting Optimal White Balance

Every color has a tonal value that tells us how bright or how dark a color is. On one end of the scale is pure white and on the other, pure black. The purpose of using a white piece of paper or any white object to set the Custom White Balance mode is to introduce a known color to the camera so that it can match what it sees on the paper to the actual color value. Before you customize the white balance, check that:

- The paper and the subject receive the same illumination.
- Your shadow is not cast over the paper.
- The paper shows through the entire frame.

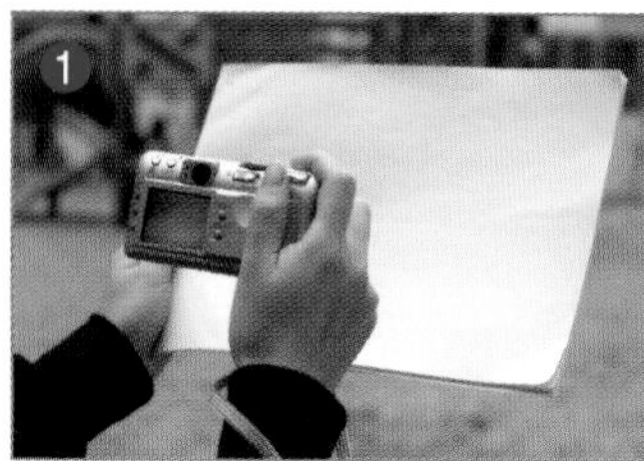

▲ Take a photo of a white piece of paper.

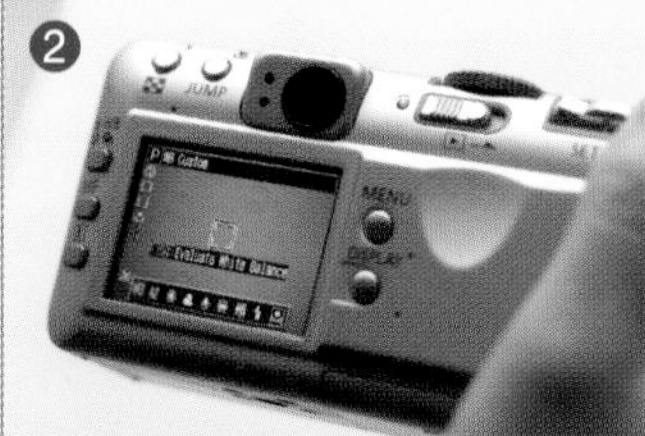

▲ Turn the dial to Custom White Balance or Manual White Balance mode, and load the photo of the white piece of paper to preset the white balance.

Choosing the Correct Mode

If you use the wrong White Balance mode, the colors in the photo will be different from the actual scene. For example, if you use the Fine mode, pictures taken under tungsten lights will appear reddish while pictures taken on a cloudy day will appear bluish.

In order to preserve the natural color of objects, you need to choose the White Balance mode to match the color temperature of the light source.

▲ White balance set for direct sunlight

▲ White balance set for incandescent lighting

Using White Balance in Landscape Photography

By experimenting with the White Balance modes on your camera, you can change the colors of your landscape photos, giving them a different ambience and mood.

The Incandescent mode adds a bluish tint to photos taken at dawn, giving them a cool look. ▶

The Flash mode adds a warm orange tone to a photo. It can be used to enhance the glow of the rising or setting sun. ▶

By selecting the Custom mode and programming the camera to perceive a colored piece of paper as white, you can produce some unusual landscape photos. In this photo, the white balance was customized using a yellow piece of paper. ▶

c h e c k l i s t

Chapter 2 | Advanced Features

- Use angled lighting for a more three-dimensional effect.
- Avoid direct light and backlighting.
- Try taking pictures of people and objects on cloudy days or in the shade.
- Note that the time of day will affect the colors in your shot.
- Turn off the flash if you don't need it.
- Use a diffuser, omni-bounce, reflector, or everyday objects such as a piece of tissue to soften the flash, if necessary.
- Take a profile shot if you are using a flash to shoot your subject in low light. This will prevent the red-eye syndrome.
- Consider using the Black-and-White and Sepia modes for a change of style.
- When shooting close-ups of small objects, remember not to get closer than your camera's minimum focusing distance.
- Try using the Continuous Shot function to shot fast-moving subjects and action sequences.
- Be sensitive to the light source's color temperature and adjust the white balance if necessary.

40 Digital Photography Techniques

Chapter 3

Photographing People

People as subjects are often the most fascinating and difficult to capture in photography. Besides fussing over the usual things, such as focus, exposure, lighting, placement, and color, a good portrait photographer must be able to capture the character and personality of the person in the shot.

For novice photographers, taking photos of family and friends is the easiest and most rewarding way to start photographing people. In this chapter, let's begin by learning to take photos of your loved ones and the people around you.

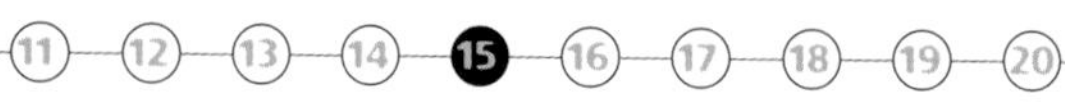

15 Taking Better People Photos

This section focuses on the essential skills and techniques that you will find useful for taking all kinds of people shots. It also looks at the common mistakes made by beginners and shows you how to avoid them. We will cover such topics as background, pose, gaze, lighting, angle of view, and group photos. I hope that by the end of this section you will be able to take better photos.

Take Close-Ups

When taking photos of people, it is important to simplify the background so as to keep the focus on the subject. Taking close-ups of people will minimize a cluttered background and maintain the viewers' focus on the subject.

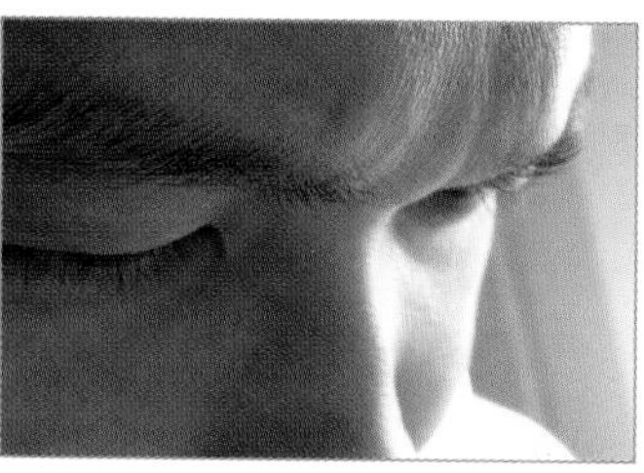

▲ Portrait shots need not include the entire face. You can study the subject's face and take a close-up of his most striking feature.

▲ Close-ups keep the person as the center of attention.

Make the Subject Feel Comfortable

People naturally tense up in front of the camera and start standing *properly* for the shoot. You should encourage your subjects to relax and adopt a pose that they feel comfortable with. It helps if you are friendly, sociable, and enthusiastic about taking their photos. This will produce more natural photos and make the photo shoot a lot more enjoyable for everyone.

▲ You can only get such a shot if the subject feels comfortable around you.

Instead of shoving the camera in your subject's face, break the ice with an introduction and some lighthearted conversation. Because you can get great candid shots while your subject is chatting, laughing, or in the midst of doing something, you have to develop a discerning eye for candid moments, and learn to jump on photographic opportunities immediately.

Focus on the Eyes

The saying that the eyes are the windows to the soul may seem overworked and clichéd, but it really applies to portraiture. A subject's gaze focuses our attention and is undoubtedly the most important element in a portrait. Perhaps it is because of this that many novices take photos with the subject looking straight at the camera. These front profile shots are common—too common, in fact—but they do not bring out the best in some subjects.

▲ Focus on your subject's eyes to capture her emotions and mental state.

Some people have more photogenic side profiles. Having such a person turn his head at a 45° angle would capture his features in a better light. Remember to keep your focus on the eye closest to the camera in order to draw your viewer's interest.

▲ Get your subject to turn his head at a 45° angle if he has a good side profile.

There are many styles you can explore, but here are two of my favorites:

- Shoot at an angle of 45° from behind a subject who is looking at something else. This has the effect of implying a sense of longing and desire in the subject.
- When taking photos of two or more people, have each person look in a different direction. This has the effect of creating leading lines along their gaze, and you can get a dynamic photo as a result.

▲ Getting your subjects to look away from each other can produce an unusual composition.

Avoid Reflected Colors

If your subject is standing near a reflective, colored surface, the light hitting the surface may reflect a color cast onto the subject, creating unnatural skin tones. You should always check that your subjects are standing away from highly reflective surfaces like cars, mirrors, or metallic backgrounds.

Lighting

▶▶▶ Avoid Harsh Shadows

If the sunlight is casting shadows on the subject's face or if the lighting is making the subject look flat or two-dimensional, use a reflector to soften the light and prevent harsh shadows. Another way is to position the subject such that the subject's face is illuminated from the side. You can also use additional lighting such as a flash to fill in the shadows.

▶▶▶ Avoid Direct Light

Avoid light that shines directly on the subject. People with pronounced cheekbones, in particular, should avoid having their photos taken under the midday sun. The direct light will produce deep shadows under their eyes and cheeks. It will also make them squint. Photos taken on cloudy days or in the shade are most ideal because the light is softer and more flattering on the face. When taking photos in the shade, however, you have to avoid having shadows cast over the subject's face.

▲ A subject placed under the shade of a tree can end up with shadows on his face.

▶▶▶ Oblique or Side Lighting

Oblique or side lighting can add contours and depth to your subject's face. But overdoing it can produce harsh shadows and make the eyes appear sunken.

▶▶▶ Backlighting

Backlighting is a good way to emphasize the form and shape of your subject and separate him or her from the background. Backlighting is perfect for taking silhouettes of buildings, objects, and people.

▲ Silhouettes taken at sunset

An installation piece inside an art gallery provided a great opportunity for a silhouette shot. In case you are wondering, the sun that you see in the picture is the installation art. ▶

Background

▶▶▶ Simplifying the Background

In situations where you have to include the background, try keeping it as simple as possible. Cluttered or messy backgrounds make for confusing photos, drawing attention away from the people in the photos. To further minimize the background, the light hitting the background should ideally be slightly dimmer than the light illuminating the subject.

Chapter 3

▶▶▶ Shooting Meaningful Backdrops

On the other hand, the background need not always be removed or kept simple. A setting that reflects the character and personality of the subject is more meaningful and will strengthen the appeal of the image. Try to take a shot with the subject assuming a natural expression and pose in her natural surroundings. You should check that the surroundings do not overpower the subject visually.

▲ A photo like this captures the character and personality of the subject.

The Focus Lock feature is great for shooting this sort of image. For instance, if you want the subject to be in focus, but not right in the center of the photo and blocking most of the background, press the shutter-release button lightly to focus on the subject first. Then move to the side to show more of the background.

Body Shape

Many people are dissatisfied with their body and the way they look in photos. But the camera can minimize these flaws when in the hands of a skilled photographer. The popular refrain that the camera doesn't lie is really a lie. The camera lies all the time.

If you shoot your subjects from a flattering angle, you can change the appearance of their body. Taking photos of overweight people from the side, for example, will make them look slimmer. Other techniques include taking photos of underweight people from the front, tall people at eye level, and short people from below.

▲ Photo of a short person taken from below

▲ Photo of a short person taken from above

Ⓥ Group Photos

Sometimes you will have one or two people who close their eyes or look the other way in group photos. There are two things you could do to alleviate this problem. Get everyone to look at the camera and instead of just taking one photo, take a few photos in succession and choose the best one. Alternatively, instead of lining everyone up for a posed shot, try taking photos of the group while everyone's carrying on with their activities.

▲ Take a few shots in succession and choose the best one.

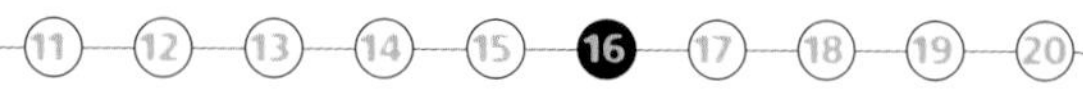

16 Changing the Camera Distance and Angle

In this section, you will discover how the distance and angle of the camera can make a subject look diminutive or powerful.

Camera-to-Subject Distance

Changing the camera-to-subject distance will change the perspective in an image. As the camera moves closer to the subject, the subject appears to increase in size relative to the background. As you move farther away from the subject, the subject becomes smaller relative to the background and the focus is shifted to the background or another part of the photo.

▲ A long shot emphasizes the background in the photo.

▲ A full body shot emphasizes both the subjects and the background. .

▲ A shot from the waist up gives more emphasis to the subjects.

▲ A shot from the chest up removes most of the background.

▲ A close-up gives the viewer a feeling of intimacy.

Camera Angle

The camera angle refers to the position at which the camera is aimed at the subject. The most common angle is at the eye level of the subject. You can also take the photo from above or below the subject's eye level. You should experiment and practice with different angles to find the angle that best enhances your subject.

In most photos of people, especially babies, the photographer takes the photo at the subject's eye level. This gives the viewer a sense of closeness and familiarity with the subject. Shooting from above or below the subject's eye level creates completely different effects. Shooting from above makes the subject appear small and diminutive, while shooting from below makes the subject look strong and powerful.

▲ Eye level: creates a sense of closeness and familiarity.

▲ Below eye level: subject appears strong and powerful.

▲ Above eye level: subject appears diminutive and weak.

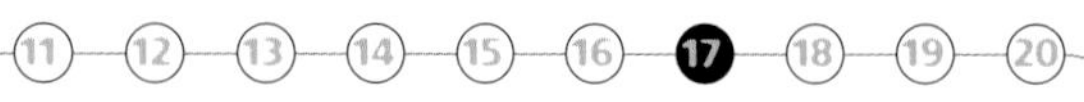

17 Using Selective Focus

When taking photos of people, you have to decide if the background is central to the theme of your photo. Is it a scenic spot or an important landmark? Does it say something about the subject? For portrait shots, many photographers choose to blur the background to keep the point of interest on the subject and create a soft, dreamy look. This technique is called selective focusing and there are a few ways of doing it.

Adjusting the Aperture

Set your camera to the Aperture Priority mode if you have a manual or semiautomatic camera, and open up the aperture as much as possible in order to get a shallow depth of field and a blurred background. Once you have set the camera to the desired aperture value, the camera will automatically adjust the shutter speed for the appropriate exposure.

If your camera is fully automatic, you can activate the Character mode or Portrait mode to create the same effect.

▲ Compare the range of focus between a shot taken with a big aperture (left image: *f*/2.0) and one shot with a small aperture (right image: *f*/8.0).

▲▶ Examples of selective-focus photography.

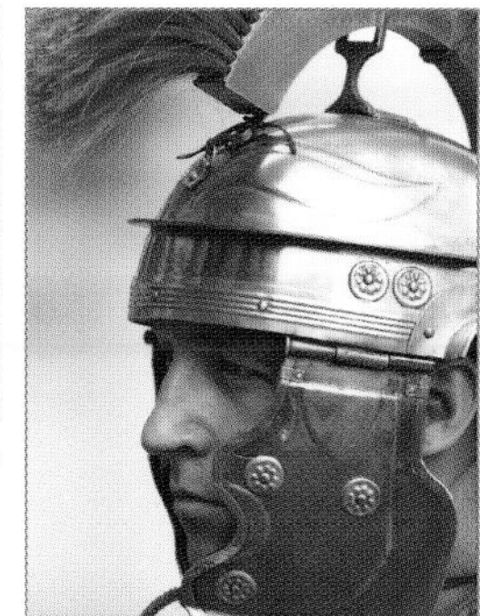

Using a Telephoto Lens

Another way of shooting selective-focused photos is to use a telephoto lens. Compared to wide-angle lenses, telephoto lenses have longer focal lengths and shallower depth of field. If you are using a zoom lens, zoom in to the telephoto range of the lens or set your camera to the Telephoto setting. For example, if you are using the ubiquitous 35–105mm zoom lens, set the lens to 70mm or above.

If you are using an automatic camera, you can selectively focus by setting the camera to the Close-Up Scene mode and zooming in to the Telephoto setting.

▲ A comparison of selective-focused photos taken using a wide-angle and a telephoto lens.

Using Selective Focus with Compact Digital Cameras

With a single-lens reflex (SLR) digital camera, you can preview the selective-focus effect directly through the viewfinder, which gives you a lot of creative control. This is not possible with compact digital cameras where everything appears in focus all the time, regardless of the settings you choose. To get the best selective-focus effects using compact digital cameras, follow these steps:

- If you are shooting macro close-ups, set your camera to the Macro mode or Close-Up mode and check that you do not go closer than the minimum focusing distance of the lens.
- Open up the aperture (small *f*-number) by selecting the Portrait mode.
- When using a zoom lens, zoom into the telephoto range of the lens or set the camera to Telephoto mode.
- When taking a photo, the distance between you and the subject should be closer than the distance between the subject and the background.

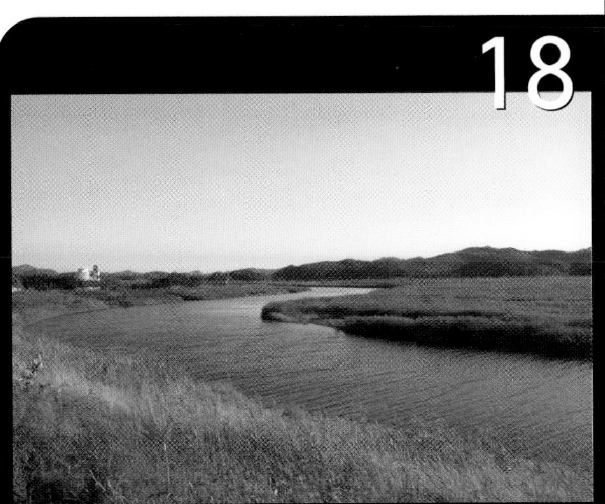

18

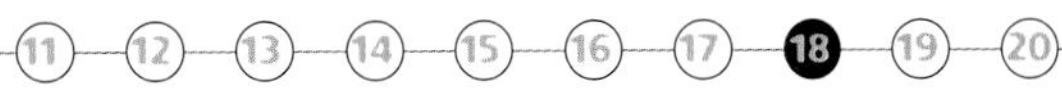

Photographing Children

Children make great subjects for photos because they are active and lively and don't freeze up in front of the camera. At the same time, it is not easy to take their photos because they can be mischievous and restless. In this section, we will look at some time-tested techniques that will help you capture photos of children.

Use Fast Shutter Speeds

To prevent motion blur, you should always set your camera to the fastest shutter speed possible. On an automatic camera, you should set it to the Sports mode or Fast Action mode, which use a fast shutter speed to capture action shots.

If you can set the shutter speed on your camera, use a shutter speed between 1/250 and 1/1000 second when taking pictures of children. If you are at a sporting event, you should use shutter speeds of between 1/500 and to 1/2000 second.

▲ Fast shutter speeds freeze the movement of fast-moving children.

Ⓥ Light Sensitivity (ISO) and Shutter Speeds

When the lighting is poor, fast shutter speeds are not feasible, as the image will be underexposed. To properly expose the image while using a fast shutter speed, the solution is to make the camera more sensitive to light (ISO). Most digital cameras support ISO ratings of 50, 100, 200, 400, 800, and 1600. The interval between these ratings (between ISO 50 and 100, for instance) is 1 stop—a term used to descibe intervals in aperture and shutter speed.

If you increase the ISO from 100 to 400, you are effectively increasing the sensitivity by 2 stops. If you keep the aperture and the exposure constant, you can increase the shutter speed by as much as 2 stops when taking a photo. For example, a picture taken at an ISO of 100 at *f*/2.0 and 1/60 second, and a photo take at an ISO of 400 (a difference of 2 stops) at *f*/2.0 and 1/250 second, have the same exposure. The downside of increasing the ISO is that your photos will have more electronic noise or graininess. Therefore, you have to strike a compromise between sharpness and graininess when you adjust the ISO.

Shoot at Their Level

If you take photos of children from above, their heads will look overly large while their legs will appear short and stubby. Another disadvantage is that you can't avoid a cluttered floor in your image. The trick is to shoot from the child's eye level, or be level with the part of the child's body you are photographing. Get down to child's level if you want great results.

▲ Get down to the child's level.

Use the Continuous Shot Feature

The Continuous Shot feature on your camera allows you to capture a child's sequence of actions. I would suggest that you take three to five continuous shots and then select the ones you like. As usual, check that you are shooting with adequate lighting and the appropriate shutter speed or Scene mode.

▲ Use Continuous Shot to capture the best moments.

Use Selective Focusing

Use selective focusing to keep the focus and attention on your child, especially if you are shooting in a crowded place. To get a good selective-focused photo using a semiautomatic camera, you should take the photo from a distance using the Telephoto mode or by setting the zoom lens to its telephoto range.

For example, if your camera has a 35–105 zoom, set the lens to between 80mm and 100mm. Next, open the aperture to its maximum to create a shallow depth of field and use a shutter speed of 1/250 second or faster. Finally, focus the camera on the child and press the shutter. If you are using an automatic camera, you can get the same effect by setting it to the Portrait mode.

▲ Use a telephoto lens to focus the attention on the child.

Use Simple Props

Simple props like toys will keep the child occupied and happy so that you can take natural shots of him playing and laughing. Movable props also help to make the photos livelier. For example, soap bubbles will light up the child's face and add an aesthetic quality to the picture.

▲ A prop does not always have to be a toy. Soap bubbles work wonders!

▲ In this photo, wooden tubs and a cute cap are used to create the country theme.

Compile a Photo Journal

One of the best ways to capture a child's growing years is to start a photo journal as opposed to 100 percent posed shots. Instead of focusing entirely on the child's activities, which most parents do, take some photos that illustrate the close bond between parent and child. It will make the album all the more special for the family, even years after the child has grown up. To take documentary photos, always have the camera on hand, and anticipate and position yourself for a shot even before it happens.

▲▶ Include family and friends in your shots, and have a diversity of themes.

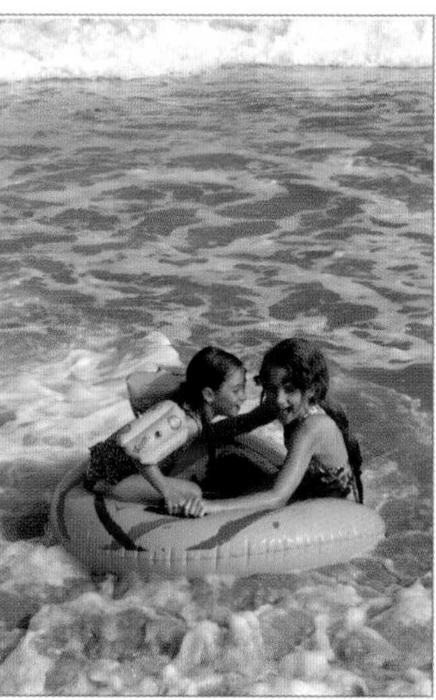

Ⓥ Close-Up Shots of Newborn Babies

Unaware of their surroundings, newborn babies are not afraid or self-conscious in front of the camera, making them great subjects for macro photography. Bear in mind that you don't have to photograph the baby's face all the time. Try taking close-up shots of its tiny nose, eyes, hands, or feet using the Macro mode for something different. Don't activate the flash when you are near the baby, though. Use a separate light source or move to a place with sufficient light instead.

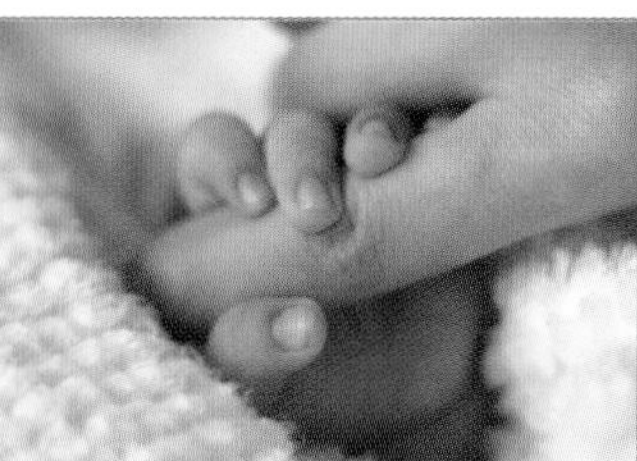

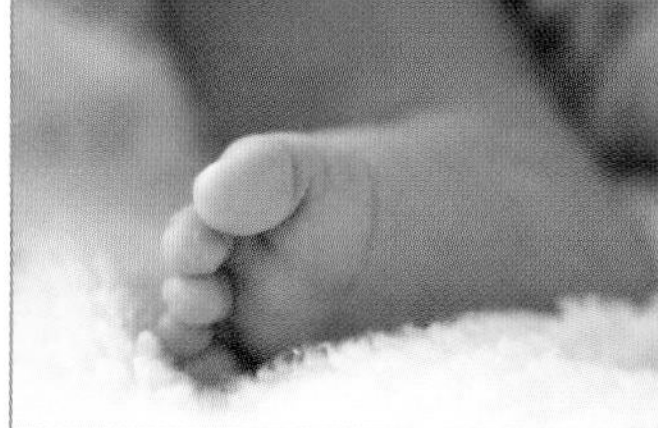

▲ Check the focusing distance of your macro lens before taking close-ups like these.

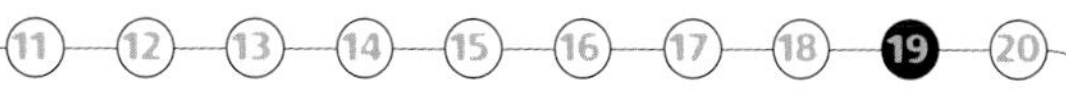

19 Shooting Self-Portraits

With film cameras, shooting self-portraits is a hit-or-miss affair. You point the camera at yourself, press the shutter-release button, and start praying hard that the photos will turn out well.

With digital cameras, you can check the self-portrait you took right away and adjust the camera position until you get it right. The odds of shooting a good self-portrait are better on a digital camera, and this is definitely a plus point when you are traveling alone.

Handheld Self-Portraits

The fastest way to take a self-portrait is to hold the camera in both hands, stretch your arms way out with the camera directed toward you, and click the shutter-release button. The challenge is to keep the camera level and get your entire face in the picture. It will be easier if your camera has a rotating lens or LCD so that you can see yourself in the LCD as you compose the shot.

▲ Practice makes perfect.

▶▶▶ Camera Angle

Instead of holding your camera straight out to shoot an eye-level photo all the time, hold it straight up or straight below for a completely different point of view.

If you are using a wide-angle lens, some distortion may be expected because of the design of wide-angle lenses. However, you can minimize distortion by zooming in slightly to a narrower angle. For example, if you are using a 35–105mm zoom lens, you should set it to 50mm.

▲ Self-portraits are mostly taken with the camera held straight out at eye-level.

▲ Holding the camera straight up will capture the scene below, making the image appear small and enclosed.

◀ Holding the camera straight below will capture the space above, making the image appear wide and open.

▶▶▶ Facial Expression

Most people stick to a single expression in all their photos. Some like to look cool and nonchalant, while others are always smiling in their photos. Practice taking your self-portraits with different expressions to convey different moods.

▲ Somber or happy? You decide.

Reflections as Self-Portraits

Try taking a picture of your reflection on a reflective surface like a mirror or a car mirror, a shiny glass, or a plate. You will capture a portrait of yourself as a photographer—a side that you don't get to see often.

▲ Mirrors or car mirrors are commonly used when taking self-portraits.

▲ Irregular reflections can produce artistic results.

Self-Portraits of a Group

Using a rotating lens or LCD, you can shoot group portraits easily. As you get better at shooting self-portraits, you may even be able to compose a shot that includes you, your companions, and the scene or landmark behind.

▲ A couple's self-portrait

Using a Tripod

For outstanding self-portraits, I recommend that you use a tripod. A heavy tripod gives great support but is not easy to move around with. Since most digital cameras are rather light, you can consider using a mini- or tabletop tripod instead.

Using a tripod and the camera's Self-Timer mode, you can compose the photo to include the background. Set the timer to 10 seconds or longer to give yourself enough time to position yourself in the frame after pressing the shutter-release button. Try out different expressions and compositions for more experimental photos.

▲▶ Using a tripod allows you to look in different directions and include the background in the photo.

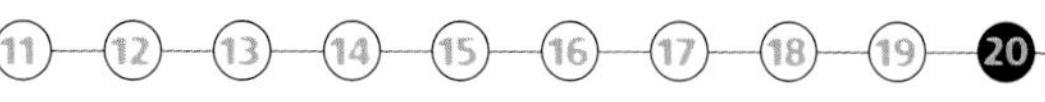

20 Using Light

In this section, I will highlight a few common lighting techniques and mistakes associated with photographing people with a digital camera. You will learn when to use the Auto Flash mode or Slow Sync mode and how white balance affects skin tones. This section does not cover everything you need to know about lighting, as most of those techniques are covered in Chapter 2.

Flash

If there is insufficient light, you can use the camera's built-in flash to light the scene. Flash can also be used indoors to freeze the actions of people who are moving.

▶▶▶ Auto Flash Mode

The Auto Flash mode is good for close-up photos or portraits that exclude the background. On the other hand, if you take a wide-angle shot in the Auto Flash mode, there is a high chance that you will overexpose the foreground subject while underexposing the background.

▶▶▶ Slow Sync Mode or Night Flash

To avoid a harsh, unnatural lighting effect, set the Flash mode to Slow Sync mode rather than Auto Flash mode. After the shutter-release button is pressed, the Slow Sync mode opens the shutter or activates the CCD long enough for the CCD to receive enough light to properly expose the image. This mode is wonderful for shooting stationary subjects, but you will need a tripod. If you want a more natural and softer look, bounce the light off a reflector or a low ceiling.

▲ You risk overexposing the foreground subject while underexposing the background in Auto Flash mode.

▲ Slow Sync mode lets in enough light to expose the background properly.

▲ Bouncing the flash off a low ceiling gives the room a soft lighting that is very forgiving of the subject's skin blemishes and flaws.

Image Color and Skin Tone

In Chapter 2, we learned that different light sources affect the color balance of the photo differently. When it comes to shooting portraits, choosing the right lighting is particularly important, as a wrong skin tone is very obvious to the eye.

In general, you can use incandescent lights to create a warm and cozy feel, as they give the image an orange tint, while candles are good for creating a warm and romantic atmosphere. Halogen lamps, normally used in art galleries and exhibitions, will enhance the skin tone of your subject, but fluorescent lights will cast a bluish tint, making the subject look pale and the mood cold.

▲ Experiment with different types of indoor lighting to create different effects.

White Balance

The Custom White Balance mode is calibrated to compensate for the color temperature of a light source, so that a white piece of paper will always appear white in the image regardless of the color cast thrown by the light source. The Custom White Balance mode is useful if you want to ensure accurate color reproduction. But if you want to preserve the original tint of the light source and the atmosphere it creates, use the Auto White Balance mode instead.

▲ Use the Auto White Balance mode to preserve the color of the lighting in your image.

▲ Using the Custom White Balance mode to remove the color cast did not capture the ambience of the location.

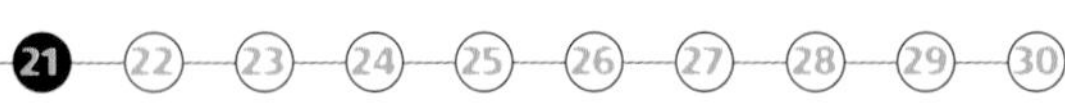

21 Manipulating Filters

Filters are placed in front of a lens to reduce glare, highlight certain hues, or create optical effects in images. There are also filters for protecting the lens. There are many filters on the market, but in this section, we will only look at those most suitable for use in people photography. You should note that you cannot attach filters to most automatic cameras. In other words, this feature is only available in mid- to high-end cameras.

About Filters

In the past, filters were often used with traditional film cameras, but their importance has declined in the computer age. Now, any photo or image can be digitally altered to create similar filter effects (and many more) through image-editing software such as Photoshop.

However, filters remain popular with some photographers who want to see the effect in the viewfinder and create a composition in harmony with the scene. In addition, the effects created by such filters as the neutral density (ND) filter and cross star filters cannot be easily reproduced using image-editing software.

How to Use a Filter

If there are grooves on the lens housing, you can attach the filter by screwing it on. With most digital cameras, you will need to attach a lens adapter before you can attach the filter.

▲ Only a lens adapter made by the manufacturer of your digital camera will be compatible with your camera.

Filters for Shooting Portraits

▶▶▶ Polarizing (PL) Filter

This filter works in two ways. It reduces the glare or reflection from reflective surfaces like glass or water, enabling you to take sharper and clearer photos. It also gives your photos better contrast and color saturation when you are shooting color photos. The filter is great for capturing sharp, vivid photos of both people and landscape in the same frame.

To use a PL filter, rotate the filter on its mount until you get the desired effect. This is easy with a digital SLR camera where you can see the effect directly through the viewfinder.

With a compact digital camera, you can't preview the effect because the lens and the viewfinder are not connected. But you can work around this problem with some ingenuity. First, place the PL filter in front of the viewfinder and rotate it until you get the desired effect. Then, without rotating the filter any more, attach it to the lens. This method will give you some idea of the filter's effect on your image, but you need some practice to get it right.

▲ Photos shot with the PL filter tend to be underexposed, so you should raise the exposure by 1/3 stop.

▶▶▶ Neutral Density (ND) Filter

The ND filter reduces the amount of light that enters the lens. In other words, it reduces the brightness of a scene. This filter is useful if you want to have a shallow depth of field when shooting in bright daylight.

As you know by now, you need to shoot with a large aperture in order to get a shallow depth of field. But this is impossible when you shoot in bright daylight, because no matter how fast you set the shutter speed, the aperture will remain small in order to compensate for the increased amount of light coming through.

With a small aperture, the depth of field will be too deep and you will be unable to take selective-focused shots. With this filter, you can reduce the scene's brightness without changing its color, thus allowing you to open up the aperture.

▲ Without the ND filter, the background will also be in focus.

▲ With the ND filter, we can open up the aperture to take selective-focused photos.

▶▶▶ Soft Filter

This filer gives a soft, blurry look to your photos, similar to Photoshop Element's Blur effect. It is excellent for creating a dreamy, romantic mood, which is why this filter is commonly used in wedding photography.

▲ Photo taken without the Soft filter

▲ Photo taken with the Soft filter

▶▶▶ Cross Star or Starburst Filter

This filter has crosshatch marks on the surface that flare light rays coming through the lens into a given number of fixed lines away from the source point. The effect of this filter is most obvious when used in night scenes with street lamps or incandescent lights. As a rule, the smaller and more intense the light source, the more pronounced is the effect in the photo. This filter is great for creating a romantic ambience in photos.

▲ Photo taken without the cross star filter

▲ Using the cross star filter gives a dreamy effect to the photo

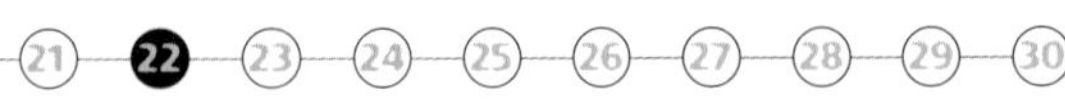

Chapter 3

22 Taking Pictures of Weddings

A wedding is a joyous occasion and a great photo opportunity for photography enthusiasts. But it is not easy to take good wedding pictures and this is why professional wedding photographers are often paid handsomely. The main challenge in wedding photography is in capturing all the important moments and getting all the shots right the first time. In this section, you will learn to prevent or overcome the problems you may face in taking wedding shots.

Memorize the Schedule

Weddings are a bustle of activity, and the bride and groom together with their entourage are constantly moving from one activity or location to another. To make sure that you capture all of the important moments, you have to memorize the wedding schedule in advance.

At the same time, you should consider the lighting conditions and general environment of the various locations and plan ahead. Once you know the schedule by heart, you can move on to the next location before the entourage and look for a good position to take the shot. On the wedding day itself, you should of course bring the schedule just in case you forget the time and location.

▲ If you know the wedding schedule, you can get to the next location before everyone else and find a good spot to take the next shot.

Be Well Equipped

Since a wedding is a once-in-a-lifetime event, you should be well equipped for the shoot. This is especially so if you promised the bride or groom to be their backup photographer. The items that you must bring are an extra battery, perhaps even the battery charger if the event will take the whole day, memory cards, an external flash if you have one, and a tripod. As an added precaution, you should also test your camera equipment a day or two before the shoot.

Arrive Early

There are two reasons why you should arrive early. First of all, you will need time to set up your equipment, take some test shots to get the exposure right, and explore the location. Secondly, being early lets you capture pre-event activities that the couple may want to show their friends. As to how early you could be there, you should consult the couple.

Apply the Principles of Action Photography

All the rules for action photography, such as using a large aperture, fast shutter speed, and tripod apply. See Technique 13 on action photography. You should note that, unlike action shots of fast-moving objects which will require the use of a semiautomatic camera, people at weddings generally move more leisurely, giving you a fair chance of success at shooting weddings with automatic cameras.

Another useful technique for taking action shots, regardless of your camera type, is to pre-focus on a specific spot that you know the subject will go past. In wedding photography, this technique is most frequently used to take pictures of a wedding couple walking down the aisle.

▲ Pre-focus on a spot by pressing down your shutter-release button halfway and releasing it only when the couple reaches the spot

▲ Although this shot would look better by moving closer to exclude the bride, whose back is facing the camera, the photographer chose to take the shot anyway because by the time he moved in, everyone might have moved off. Another consideration is that the photo can be cropped later to exclude the bride and the singer.

Using Flash

At one point or another, the wedding festivities will take place indoors, and you will need to use a flash to take indoor action shots. If you take formal group shots indoors, you will find that you need to move farther away to include the entire group in the picture, and this could render your built-in flash ineffective because the distance is beyond the flash's range. The solution is to attach an external flash unit to your camera. If that's not possible, check the flash distance of your built-in flash and try to keep within the flash range.

▶ Using the flash to freeze actionn

Another important factor to remember when using the flash is to make sure that it doesn't fire when the professional photographer is taking a shot, as this will ruin his picture. It helps to remember that the wedding couple paid the professional photographer big bucks for the best possible pictures, and he should be given the consideration to do his job properly.

Posed Shots

If the schedule allows, for example, you are the bridesmaid and you have a private moment with the bride, you can take posed shots. When taking posed shots, there are some standard poses that you can try out. A popular pose is to have the bride or groom looking into the dressing mirror.

When taking posed shots of the bride, you should study her wedding gown, jewelry, and hairdo and look for the defining characteristics. With a low-back dress, you can take a shot of the bride's back view with or without her looking back over her shoulder. For very long trains, try arranging the train in a semicircle around the bride so that it flows and doesn't look like she's dragging it along. You may also want to use the soft filter to create the dreamy, fantastic look when taking posed shots.

Photojournalistic Shots

On the other hand, if the wedding couple and almost everyone else are too busy to pose for you, you can take photojournalistic pictures. Photojournalism is a photography style much like the pictures you see in the newspapers. This style, often in black and white, is great for documenting a wedding to tell a story.

Taking photojournalistic pictures instead of formal shots at weddings may often be a better idea for photography hobbyists. This is because the couple and the entourage will not have time to work out their pose for you and you will end up taking pictures of the same pose as everyone else. While the couple and the official photographer are busy with the formal shots, take the opportunity to take alternative shots. For example, you can take pictures of the wedding invitation set against some decorative elements, the wedding couple figurine on the wedding cake, or the champagne glasses.

▲ Photojournalistic shot

At times when you are unable to take good pictures of the wedding couple (for example, when you can't zoom in far enough when the couple is exchanging their vows), you should also explore alternative subject matter.

Checklist

- Go closer.
- Make the subject feel comfortable.
- Focus on the eyes.
- Consider the lighting's effect on the subject's features.
- Decide if you should simplify the background or shoot meaningful backdrops.
- Consider the effect the camera position will have on your subject's body shape.
- Take more than one shot for group photos to make sure you have everyone looking at the camera.
- Use the Portrait Scene mode, open up the aperture, or zoom in to blur the background.
- When taking photos of children, use a fast shutter speed, go down to their level, use the Continuous Shot function, and use simple props.
- Try taking self-portraits of just yourself or with company.
- Use the flash to freeze action.
- Use the Slow Sync mode or Night Flash to keep both your subject and background illuminated when taking a shot at night.
- Adjust the white balance if you do not like the color cast on your subject's skin.
- Use a polarizing (PL) filter to reduce glare or reflection.
- To blur out the background when taking a shot in bright daylight, use the neutral density (ND) filter to reduce the amount of light entering the camera.
- Use the soft filter for a dreamy look.
- Try using the cross star or starburst filter when shooting on the streets at night to create starbursts for a romantic ambience.

40 Digital Photography Techniques

Chapter 4

Shooting Landscapes

While people photography is about reacting fast enough to capture the right moment, landscape photography is mostly about waiting for the right moment. I say mostly because, unless you are on the trail of a twister or some other exceptional weather phenomenon, most landscape shots are pretty static shots of nature and cityscapes.

With landscape photography, there is no hurry. You can take your time to try the different lenses, experiment with different compositions, and wait for the right light or time to shoot your photo.

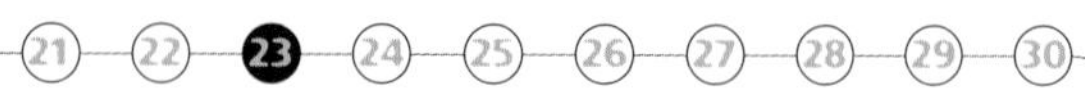

23 Landscape Photography Essentials

In order to take outstanding photos, you need to develop an eye for the beauty around you. The next time you come across a good photo, make a point to study it carefully and think about how it was shot. For landscape photography, you need to be sensitive to the light conditions, and how sunlight changes the mood of the landscape. You also need to learn how to compose well-balanced landscape shots.

Choosing a Scene

Apart from dangerous situations such as a safari photography outing, you should always get out of your car and explore your surroundings on foot in order to find the perfect scene. When a view strikes an emotional chord, you will know instinctively that you have found your subject matter. Then you should wait patiently for the perfect time, light, and weather conditions to take the photo.

▲ You must actively go in search of a good scene for your photos.

Composition Is Everything

▶▶▶ Horizontal or Vertical?

Composition is the most critical factor in landscape photography, so you should spend more time composing or trying out different compositions. It will help you to know that horizontal photos exude a sense of stability and emphasize the breadth of a scene, whereas vertical photos emphasize height and depth.

▲ A horizontal photo is used to capture the expansiveness of a scene.

▲ A vertical photo emphasizes height.

▶▶▶ Camera Angle

You should also consider the effect of the camera angle on your photo. A low angle adds vitality and dimension to the scenery, whereas a high angle gives a down-to-earth feel. With practice, you can develop a visual sense of the angles and compositions that work with certain situations.

▲ A low-angle landscape photo appears majestic and full of life.

▲ A high angle landscape photo gives an enclosed, down-to-earth feel.

▶▶▶ Balance

If the composition is unbalanced, the photo will look unattractive even if the scene is fantastic.

▲ The horizon is slanted, making the photo look unbalanced.

▲ The re-composed photo looks much better.

▶▶▶ Break Away from Convention

Conventional landscape photos place the main point of interest at the center of the frame. This sort of composition is fine, but it can be boring after a while. Try placing the subject off-center for bold and interesting effects.

▲ Think of a few different subject placements and experiment with them.

▶▶▶ Simplify the Background

A good landscape photo harmonizes the subject with its surroundings. One way of doing this is to keep the focus on the subject by simplifying the background and eliminating unnecessary elements. This is why landscape photography is an exercise in the beauty of subtraction.

▶ Remove unnecessary elements from the background to emphasize the subject.

Pan Focusing and Selective Focusing

▶▶▶ Pan Focusing

Pan focusing is a technique used frequently in landscape photography to keep the entire photo sharp and clear. The effect is achieved by using a wide-angle lens and a small aperture (*f*/8 or higher), if you are using a semiautomatic camera, to keep both the foreground and background in focus. On an automatic camera, zoom out to the wide-angle setting and select the Landscape Scene mode, which sets the focus at infinity. Pan focusing is another way of saying that the image has a deep depth of field.

▲ Use pan focusing to keep everything in sharp focus.

▶▶▶ Selective Focusing

Use the selective-focusing technique with a large aperture (*f*/2.8–*f*/4) if you want to limit the focus on a particular object. You can do this by setting your camera to Telephoto mode or, if you are using a zoom lens, setting it to 70mm or above.

Depending on the camera distance, you can also use the Portrait or Close-Up Scene modes and zoom in to the Telephoto setting to shoot a selective-focused photo.

▲ Use selective focusing to emphasize a particular object.

The Changing Light

Besides composition, light is the other key element in landscape photography. The light changes continuously throughout the day, which is why photos of the same scene taken at different times of the day will appear drastically different.

▲ Shot at dawn

You have to be sensitive to the changing light conditions in order to capture a scene with the appropriate mood. Take note of the direction of the light. In general, backlighting emphasizes the shapes and forms in the landscape, whereas oblique or side lighting tends to enhance the contours and textures of the landscape.

▲ Shot during the day

▲ Backlighting emphasizes the shape and form of the leaves.

▲▶ Shot at sunset

Using Fill Flash

Although the flash is normally used for poorly lit areas, using it to shoot objects in nature can create wonderful results. Set the Flash mode to Fill Flash mode, focus on a nearby object in the foreground and then trigger the flash. Because the light from the flash does not spread over a wide area, this will make the object in the foreground look sharp and stand out from the background.

▲▶ Using the Fill Flash to give more depth to the photo

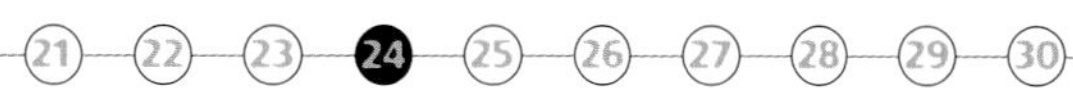

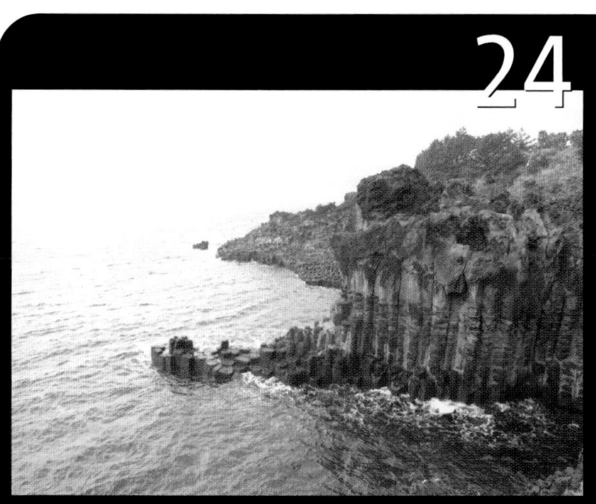

24 Taking Vacation Photos

Since the camera is the essential travel companion for travelers in the 21st century, this section is tailored to experiences that are commonly encountered by travelers. You will learn practical skills and techniques that will help you maximize the photo opportunities you will come across in your travels.

Tourist Attractions

To get a good photo of a tourist attraction, find a spot where you can get a nice angle and check that neither people nor buildings block your view. In summer months or during extended holidays, this can be difficult as you have to fight with hordes of tourists, all armed with a camera just like you. In winter months, it is much easier to get a clear shot with few or no tourists in them, and this will improve the ambience of your photos dramatically.

▶▶▶ Be Original!

Many people are familiar with famous tourist attractions through postcards and travel books without even visiting the actual location.This is because many of us take our photos from the same designated scenic spot. You should, therefore, try to shoot from a different view or incorporate the less-photographed elements in your photos to set your vacation photos apart from everyone else's.

▶ Look for a unique scene.

▶▶▶ Include More Variety

Make it a point to vary the angle and composition of your photos. You should also think about giving your photos a personal style. If you have the time, visit the same sites at night to take photos with a different mood. Some scenes or landmarks, which look plain or dull in the day due to air pollution, will look much better as night shots if they are lit up at night.

▲ Photos of world-famous sites are the highlight of travel photos.

▲ Try to take some night shots as well.

▶▶▶ Special Events

Special events are sometimes held at tourist spots or concert halls. To avoid jostling with the crowd and taking pictures of the back of people's heads, go early and find a good spot.

▲ You will need to leave your seat and get close to the performers when taking pictures at concerts.

▲ Scout the area for a good location to view the event.

People, Objects, and Locations

Although most of the photos you will take while on vacation are landscape photos, you should get a good mix of landscape photos, and photos of yourself and your travel companions, in order to capture the memories you share together.

▶▶▶ Facial Expressions

Be attentive and capture a range of expressions to document the highs and lows of your voyage.

▲ Smile for the camera.

▶▶▶ Memorable Objects or Souvenirs

Try to include street signs or other objects unique to the areas you visit in your photos. Street signs can help you remember where you have been, especially if you were on a whirlwind tour, while interesting objects make great conversation topics for your friends and family back home.

▲ Signposts help you remember where you've been.

▶▶▶ Shooting from Inside a Moving Vehicle

You will sometimes see a great view while you are inside a moving vehicle. Increase the sensitivity (ISO) of your camera to produce sharper images.

▲ Blurry motion lines in your photos

Taking Photos through a Window

- Place the camera at an angle and as close as possible to the window to cut down on reflections.
- Select the Landscape Scene mode to set the focus to infinity. If your camera is set to autofocus, it may end up focusing on the windowpane, leaving the scene a blur.

▲ Take the photo at an angle to avoid capturing the reflections on the bus window.

▲ In this shot, I did not use the Landscape Scene mode because I wanted to capture the ice crystals on the plane window.

▶▶▶ Combining Subject and Background

If you stand too close to the subject, you will neglect the background, but if you stand too far away, the subject becomes indistinguishable from the background. To give equal importance to the subject and the background, shoot at a distance and angle that will give a sense of balance between the two.

▶ In this shot, the foreground subject leads the viewer's gaze into the building in the background. This technique of using a foreground interest to lead into the background is often used to create depth in a picture and to avoid having a flat, boring composition.

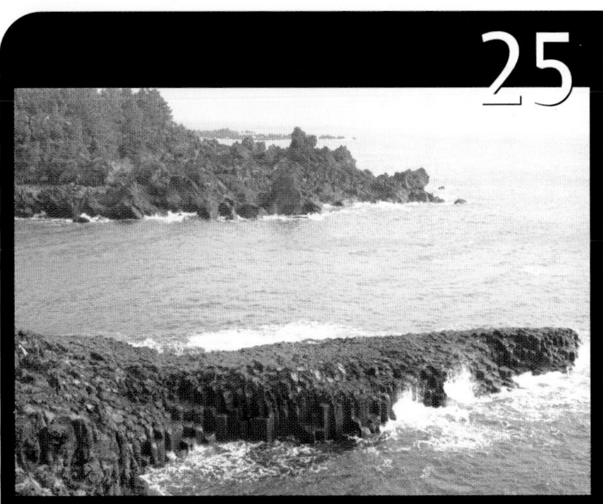

25

Rainy Day Photos

Rainy days are great for taking landscape photos because the falling rain cloaks the landscape in a shroud of mist and water, and the resulting low-contrast scene with muted colors can give a painterly quality to your photos.

In this section, you will learn how to protect your camera from the rain and how to take good photos on a rainy day.

Protecting the Camera

Digital cameras, like all electronic products, are very sensitive to moisture and humidity. You need to take extra care to protect your camera from the rain. Most people would take a shot holding the camera in one hand and an umbrella in the other. This is ineffective because strong winds can get the rain on the camera. Here are a few ways of protecting your camera from the rain:

▶▶▶ Waterproof Case

The most secure method is to use a waterproof case, which is designed for underwater photography. As such cases are very expensive, it is not the most practical solution.

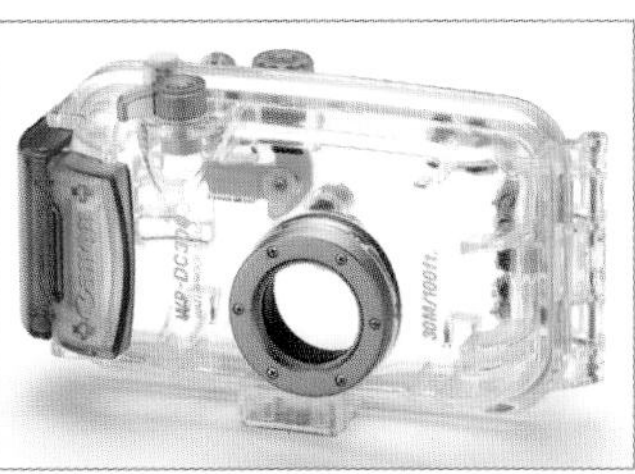

▲ Your best bet is to use a waterproof camera case, but these cases are very expensive.

Chapter 4

▶▶▶ Plastic Wrap

Take a common household plastic bag, wrap it around your camera, and make a hole in the plastic for the lens. This is an inexpensive option for amateurs.

▲ Wrapping the camera with a plastic bag

▶▶▶ Waterproof Camera Bag

Waterproof camera bags have great water-resistant capabilities and are cheap, making them effective as well as practical.

▲ Waterproof camera bags are not only great for rainy days but also for winter outings.

tip If All Else Fails...

If you just cannot shield the camera from the rain, take photos of the scene outside from inside instead.

tip Caution

For your own safety, do not go out when there is a lightning or thunderstorm.

▲ A photo shot from inside

Tips

Camera Shake

On rainy days, you may need to use a slow shutter speed due to the poor light condition. On an automatic camera, you can try shooting in the Party/Indoor Scene mode. As this increases the risk of motion blur, we recommend that you use a tripod.

Artificial Rain

If you don't like getting wet, an alternative is to use a garden hose and create artificial rain. This lets you control the rain and use it to mimic the effects of a summer downpour.

Adding Accents

If the scene is universally dark and gloomy, try to compose the shot with a brighter object in the foreground to add accents to the photo.

▲ Use flowers as accents.

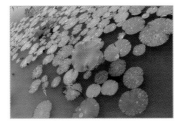

▲ Use lotus leaves as accents.

Taking Photos of Raindrops

If you want to capture the falling rain, set the scene against a dark background. Set the shutter speed between 1/250 and 1/1000 second or use the Sports Scene mode.

You can also create a rainy-day mood by taking photos of raindrops on leaves, raindrops hitting the windowpanes, or people holding umbrellas. Using selective focusing (Portrait Scene mode or Close-Up mode) and a telephoto lens, you can create a dreamy, misty effect.

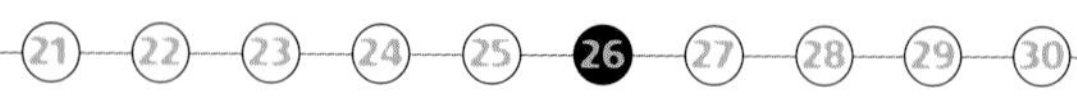

26 Snowy Day Photos

For the most part, you should take the same precautions when photographing on snowy days as you would on rainy days. There are, however, factors you need to keep in mind in addition to protecting the camera from the snow.

Battery

Apart from waterproofing your camera, you should always have an extra battery on hand. The battery will drain rapidly when out in the cold, so try to keep it warm by putting it in your pocket.

Shutter Speed

Set a shutter speed faster than 1/100 second or use the Sports Scene mode to capture the falling snowflakes. Press the shutter-release button as soon as you find the perfect balance between the subject and the falling snow.

▲ Capture the right moment with a fast shutter speed.

▲ A slow shutter speed gives a silky texture to this river, enhancing the dreamlike quality of the image.

Polarizing (PL) Filter

A clear morning or night is best for taking photos of snowy landscapes. If you have a polarizing (PL) filter, use it to enhance the contrast and saturate the colors.

▲ Use a PL filter to enhance the contrast.

Exposure

One of the most crucial factors in snow-covered landscape photography is the exposure. Because the snow is white and your camera's exposure meter is calibrated to 18 percent gray, you will get an inaccurate exposure reading if you take the reading off of the snow. If you follow this reading without adjustment, your photos will be underexposed and the snow will look gray instead of white.

This can be corrected by increasing the exposure. Although this may vary depending on the weather and the amount of snow, raising the exposure by 1/2 stop or 1 stop can usually correct the underexposure. If your camera has AEB, or Auto Exposure Bracketing mode, use it to get the best results.

▲ Exposure increased by 1 stop.

▶ For gray, urban landscapes, it may be advisable to shoot when the city is covered in snow, as the highlights from the snow will give the scene a pure, refreshing appeal.

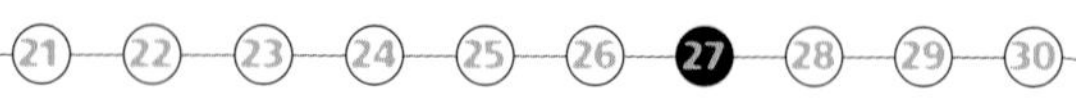

27

Night Photography

Novice photographers hesitate to take outdoor photos at night, because such photos require the use of a tripod or other accessories and it is quite difficult to get the exposure right. In this section, you will learn that it is not that hard to take stunning photos at night, capturing city lights, creating traffic light trails, and shooting photos of fireworks.

Capturing City Lights

Light sources like streetlights, automobile lights, neon signs, and brightly lit buildings or areas offer many opportunities to take photos of the city at night. With good planning, you can take captivating shots of brightly lit areas that stand out against the dark.

▶▶▶ Camera Shake

A tripod or some other on-location support is essential for night photography because it will keep your camera steady during long exposures. Professional photographers will also use a cable release or the Remote Control function on their cameras to trigger the shutter-release button. This is to prevent camera shake, which becomes more obvious on the image during long exposures. For beginners, neither the cable release nor the Remote Control function are really necessary. Just a firm but gentle press on the shutter-release button will do.

▶▶▶ Shutter Speed

You need a digital camera that supports shutter speeds of 1 second or longer.

▶▶▶ Adjusting the Exposure

Using the Automatic mode to take a photo of the city at night will produce a photo with a dark background. You can try to compensate for this by increasing the exposure using exposure compensation. Although this will make your photos brighter, you will not be able to capture the actual mood of the scene. To reproduce the brightness of the scene more accurately, set your camera to Spot Metering mode and reduce the exposure by 1/2 stop.

If you can't adjust the exposure, use the Night Landscape mode, which turns off the flash and uses a slow shutter speed to take in the city lights.

▲ Increasing the exposure under Automatic mode will make your photos too bright.

▲ Use Spot Metering mode and reduce the exposure by 1/2 stop to reproduce the actual scene.

▶▶▶ Time of Night

Night photography refers to photos taken from the moment the sun goes down to the moment the sun begins to rise. Photos taken at dawn and at dusk have a bluish tint because there is still some light in the sky. This light has a high color temperature, giving your image a bluish color cast.

For photos taken in the middle of the night, the sky appears completely black because there is no longer any light in the sky. Experiment with taking photos of the city at different times of the night.

▲ Photos taken right after the sun goes down appear bluish in tone.

▲ In photos taken in the middle of the night, the sky appears black.

Creating Traffic Light Trails

Setting the shutter speed to 2 seconds or longer in the Shutter Priority or Manual mode will allow you to capture the light streaks or trace the movement of lights from moving vehicles. This method captures the movement of light sources in a way that is not normally visible to the human eye. When photographing light trails, you should check that the scene is dim enough. If is too bright, it will cancel out the light trails in the photo.

Even if you can't set the shutter speed on your camera, you can still create this effect by using the Night Landscape Scene mode. You have to check that your camera supports shutter speeds of 2 seconds or longer, though.

▲ The light streaks brighten up the image considerably.

Cut the Noise Out

Slow shutter speeds have a tendency to add electronic noise to your photos. This can be reduced somewhat by using a low sensitivity setting, for example ISO 50 or ISO 100. On some entry-level cameras you can activate the Noise Reduction mode to cut down the noise, while on others the camera automatically processes photos taken in the Night Landscape mode to reduce noise before saving them to the memory card.

To photograph traffic light trails, position your camera where there are a lot of cars. Remember to keep a safe distance. Since you need a slow shutter speed of 2 seconds or longer, you should use a tripod or place your camera on a flat surface when taking the photo. You should also bracket your exposures for the same shot.

▲ Shot at a shutter speed of 30 seconds

Shooting Photos of Fireworks

To take photos of fireworks, you will need to bring a tripod. Once you reach the scene, check the wind direction. Because the smoke from the fireworks can get in the way of your photos, your back should always be to the oncoming wind.

To get a good composition, include people, buildings, or water in the foreground to give the viewer a sense of the location and the magnitude of the fireworks display.

On an automatic camera, you can set it to the Fireworks Show mode, which uses a slow shutter speed, responds more rapidly to the shutter-release button, fixes the focus at infinity, and turns off the flash to capture the display. Not all automatic cameras come with this mode so you should check your camera's specifications.

If you have a semiautomatic camera, you should set the shutter speed to 3 seconds or longer at most fireworks displays. Since you will never know when the climax of the display is coming, always make sure you have ample memory space and keep your attention on the fireworks right up to the end.

▲ A shutter speed of 8 seconds was used to capture several fireworks in one photo.

▲ Use a telephoto lens to fill the frame with an electrifying and impressive view of the fireworks.

▲ Focusing on the foreground has the effect of diminishing the size of the fireworks. You don't want to do this!

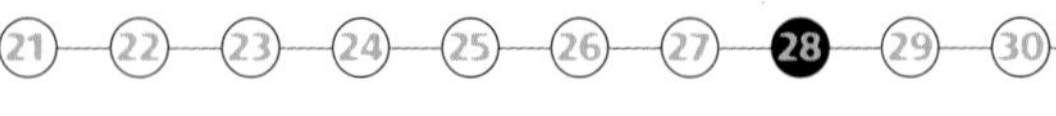

Chapter 4

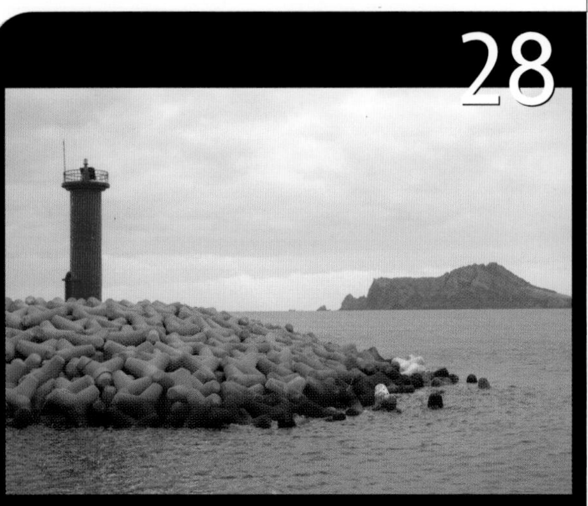

28 Capturing Sunrises and Sunsets

It is relatively easy to take good photos of sunrises and sunsets, because errors in exposure will not drastically affect the final image. This is one of the reasons why sunrises and sunsets are among the most rewarding subjects, for novice photographers. In addition, the dramatic display in the sky is there for all to see, so you will not need to venture far to take the shots.

Planning

Since you only have a short time to capture the rising or setting sun, you should plan your shot beforehand and look for a location with a clear view of the sky. The best time to shoot is about half an hour before or after the sun rises or sets. This is the time when the sky and the landscape are bathed in a warm, golden hue.

Use a Telephoto Lens

A telephoto lens is essential. With 3X zoom lenses like the 35–105mm lens, you can get a nice shot of the landscape with the sun in the background, if you set the lens to its maximum telephoto capability.

▲ Sunset taken with a 50mm lens

▲ Sunrise taken with a 50mm lens

However if you want the sun to dominate the frame, you will need a digital camera with a higher telephoto capability. Alternatively, you can use your camera's digital zoom feature and include nearby buildings or objects in your photo to make the sun look larger in comparison.

▲ Using a 200mm lens to fill the frame with the sun's orange hue

▲ This sunset was photographed using a 400mm lens. The photo includes the nearby buildings to show the sun setting on the city.

Rule of Thirds

In general, photos with the subject directly in the center look less interesting than photos with the subject off center. For example, if you are taking photos of a sunrise or sunset, divide the frame into thirds and place the sun or horizon on the lower 1/3 of the frame to emphasize the sky or the upper 1/3 of the frame to emphasize the water or land mass.

This is called the Rule of Thirds, and a more detailed discussion of this rule is found in Technique 7, "Composing a Shot." It is best to take the Rule of Thirds as a guide and a reminder to avoid placing your subject in the center in all your shots. In some instances, it may even be better to break this rule.

▲ Emphasis is placed on the ocean.

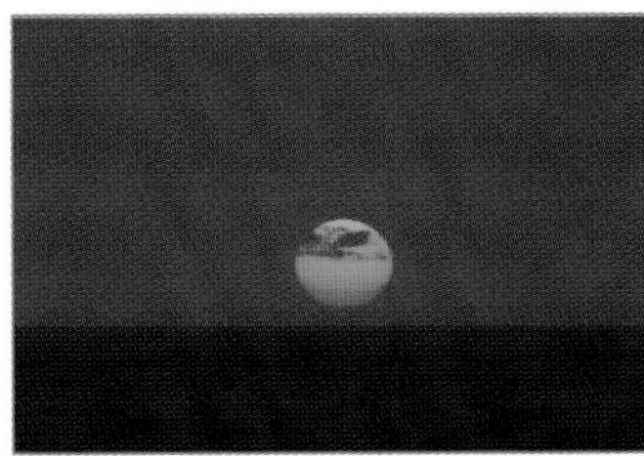

▲ Emphasis is placed on the sky.

▲ Capturing birds in flight to add movement and accents to the photo

Capturing the Changing Hues of the Sky

The sky is at its most beautiful when the sun is on the horizon. However, you can get a better range of colors in the sky when the sun has dipped below the horizon or when it is about to rise. Since the sun is not in the scene, it is also easier to get the correct exposure.

▲ At sunset, the ocean looks golden.

▲ Vibrant hues fill the sky at sunset.

Be sensitive to the changing light. At sunrise and sunset, the sky can put on a show of reflected light that dramatically lights up clouds or bathes the landscape in a warm, soft glow. The best thing about shots of sunrises and sunsets is that they are always unique. You can't take another shot with the exact same combination of cloud cover, lighting, and hue.

▲ Capturing the beauty of sunrise

▲ Capturing the beauty of sunset.

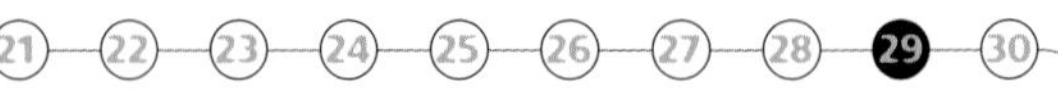

29 Creating Panoramas

In the past, panoramic photographs could only be taken with special panoramic film cameras. Today, you can take panoramic photos with a digital camera that has a Panorama mode as well. This function is particularly useful for conveying the scale and sense of openness of an expansive landscape. In this section, you will learn how to take panoramic shots and use a software program to stitch a panoramic photo on the computer.

Use the Panorama Mode

To create a seamless panorama, you should take a series of shots around a single point of rotation. In other words, you should rotate your camera around the same point when shooting left-to-right or right-to-left portions of the scenery. You can also shoot from top to bottom or bottom to top for a vertical panorama.

The LCD displays the previous shot so that you can keep your photos straight and level with the ground. The series of shots will later be stitched together to form one panoramic shot using either the proprietary stitching tool bundled with your camera or independent computer software such as Photoshop Elements.

Although panoramas are mostly shot to emphasize the grandeur of a landscape, they can also be used to bring out other elements such as people and objects.

◀ I would have had to sacrifice either the mountain or the sea if I hadn't shot this photo in panoramic format.

In this photo, the panoramic format is used to highlight the journey of the people; the landscape, in contrast, is not the main focus. Be on the lookout for opportunities to shoot such offbeat compositions!

Use a Tripod

You need a sturdy tripod in order to keep all the shots level with the ground. Depending on whether it is a horizontal or vertical sequence, always keep the camera parallel with the horizontal or vertical axis. In order to create a seamless panorama, do not move from your position while photographing. Do rotate your camera a little at a time to make sure that the shots overlap. In addition, you should not readjust the height of your tripod once you start shooting.

It is possible to shoot panoramas without a tripod, but you will need to keep your body still, your hands steady, and your movement controlled. As is to be expected, these photos will not align as well as those shot with a tripod, so you will need to rotate and crop the shots in an image-editing software.

▲ Keep your photos aligned.

Maintain the Same Exposure

When taking panoramic photos, you will be taking several photos across a wide area. Each area will have a different amount of light and shade, resulting in a slightly different exposure for each of the shots. When this happens, your panorama will appear patchy and uneven when you combine the photos.

To avoid this problem, set a fixed exposure for all the shots if your digital camera allows for manual exposure adjustment. Alternatively, set the camera to AE-Lock (Auto Exposure Lock) to ensure that exposure and white balance setting is consistent throughout. The settings are locked to that of the first image in the series after turning on the Panorama mode.

▲ Fix the exposure before taking a series of shots.

Beware of Distortion

A wide-angle lens will create slight distortions at the edge of individual shots. These subtle distortions will become noticeable when you stitch your photos together. To minimize distortion, you should zoom to the telephoto range or set your camera to the Telephoto mode.

▲ A wide-angle lens will warp the edges of the photo.

▲ Use a telephoto lens to eliminate distortion.

Overlap Photos As You Take Them

Make sure that the photos in the series overlap at the edges. The Panorama mode uses the overlapping areas to match the photos seamlessly. It is recommended that each of your photos should overlap by about 20 percent.

▲ Photos with overlapping sections

▲ Using these overlaps you can create a smooth panorama.

Combining Panoramas in the Computer

In this step-by-step example, we will show you how to create a panorama in PhotoStitch—Canon's easy-to-use software for stitching panoramas. PhotoStitch is bundled with many of Canon's digital cameras, but you can also buy it separately from Canon at a very low price.

① Start the program. Click on the Open icon and select the photos.

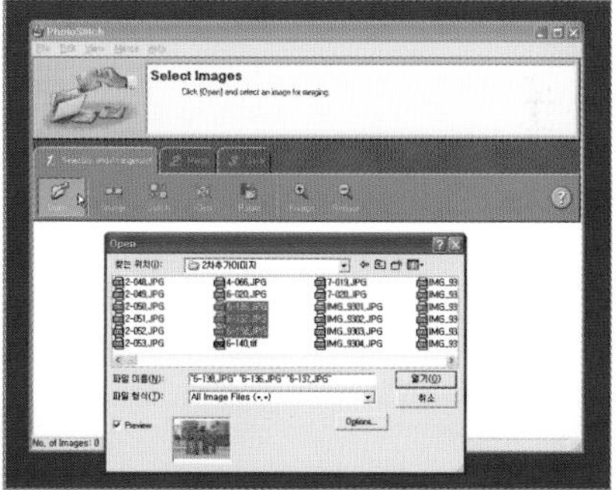

② Open the selected photos. After placing your photos in their proper order, click the Merge tab and then click the Start icon to combine the photos into a panorama.

③ Click the Save tab. You will see that a green line appears. This line is used to de-clutter your panorama.

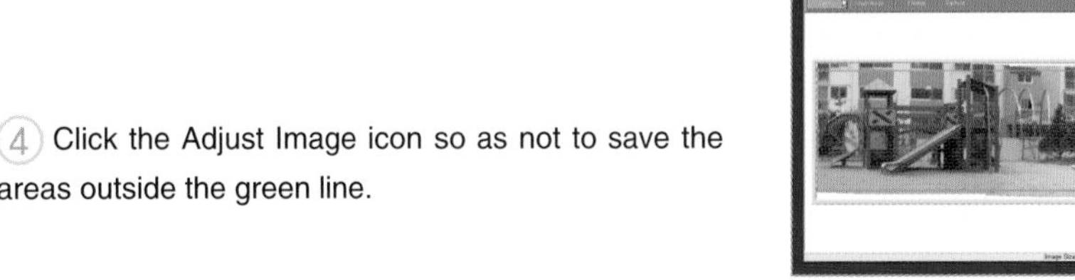

④ Click the Adjust Image icon so as not to save the areas outside the green line.

⑤ Check the Crop option and then click Save to save the panorama.

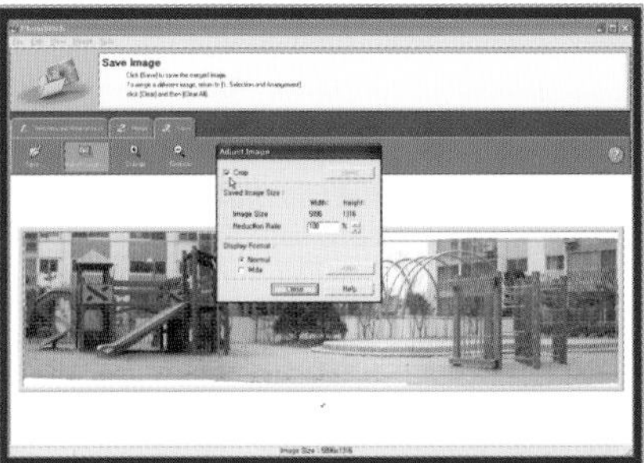

⑥ The panorama is now complete.

Checklist

Chapter 4 | Shooting Landscapes

- Explore your surroundings.
- Try out different camera angles, orientations, and styles.
- Check to see whether the composition is balanced.
- Simplify the background.
- Choose to either blur out the background or keep everything in focus.
- If a scene or landmark looks dull because of air pollution, try taking the shot when it is lit up at night.
- Go early and get a good spot when shooting events.
- When taking photos through a glass, shoot at an angle and select the Landscape Scene mode.
- Use a plastic wrap, a waterproof camera bag, or a waterproof case when shooting in the rain.
- In winter, bring an extra battery and keep the camera warm by putting it in your pocket.
- Use a polarizing filter to enhance the contrast and saturate the colors.
- Try using a slow shutter speed when taking pictures of rivers and streams to create motion streaks.
- Raise the exposure by 1/2 or 1 stop or use the Auto Exposure Bracketing mode when shooting snow scenes.
- When shooting at night, use a tripod or some other on-location support and use a shutter speed of 1 second or longer.
- Set the shutter speed to 2 seconds or longer to capture traffic streaks.
- If you can't adjust the shutter speed, try using the Night Landscape Scene mode.
- Zoom in to the sun when taking pictures of sunrises and sunsets.
- Take pictures half an hour before or after the sun rises or sets to get a better range of colors in the sky.

40 Digital Photography Techniques

Chapter 5

Experimenting with Common Themes

It is important to realize that there are no hard and fast rules to follow in photography. After you have learned the basic skills, you need to explore different themes and experiment with various scenarios in order to shoot better photos. Of course, the more practice you put into taking different kinds of photos, the better you will be at creating and handling different scenarios. In this chapter, we will look at some common photographic themes such as food, products, cars, and architecture.

30 Food Photography

Food photography is a specialized field of photography. Commercial photos of food are usually taken in a studio with a food stylist, an art director, and a professional photographer. It is, however, possible for photography hobbyists to shoot photos of food outside the studio.

Capturing the Essence

The secret to food photography is in capturing the defining characteristic of a food and making it look as delicious as possible. For instance, photos of pizza should focus on the soft, melting cheese, while photos of coffee should have a close-up shot of the aroma slowly rising out of the coffee. The idea behind food photography is to convey the taste and scent of the food to the viewer.

▲ A general shot of pizzas through the window fails to excite taste buds.

▲ Giving the cheese more emphasis makes the pizza look tempting.

▲ A cup of coffee with a frothy topping looks rich and enticing.

A common mistake in taking photos of non-solid food is to place the camera so close that the broth or sauce gets splashed onto the lens. When taking such close-ups, keep the camera a safe distance away.

▲ Make sure that the oil does not get on the lens.

▲ Avoid splashes from soups or broths.

Vary the Angle and Composition

A well-composed photo showing part of the food can be more appetizing than a shot showing the food and the entire plate. In photography, less is often more, and you can create a stronger impact by showing just a portion of the food. The objective is to keep the point of interest on what matters most. This varies with the characteristics of the food, the table setting, and the background.

When taking photos of food (especially those with good form and color), use selective focusing to blur the background clutter. By opening up the aperture (small *f*-number) or using the Macro mode, you can focus on the food and blur the background.

▲ Only a section of this jar of cherries was photographed to emphasize the redness of the cherries.

▲ A close-up showing the top of the cake emphasizes the splendid presentation and vibrant colors.

▲ Blurring the table gives emphasis to the food in the photo.

For food with little form or color, on the other hand, it is better to introduce accents such as rising steam or to keep decorative elements like crockery, table setting, and background in focus. In the shot on the right, coffee beans were used as accents for an otherwise dull shot.

▶ The shot of coffee beans is included to relay the message of freshness and use of quality ingredients.

As a guide, try to vary the food presentation, camera angle, and composition in your shots and also consider enhancing your shots using natural ingredients or artificial props.

▲ Use a large aperture of *f*/2.0 or Macro mode to fade the table into the background.

▲ A background sheet and a sprinkling of chocolate powder complete the look.

▲ Spraying water on the oranges adds a refreshing touch to the photo.

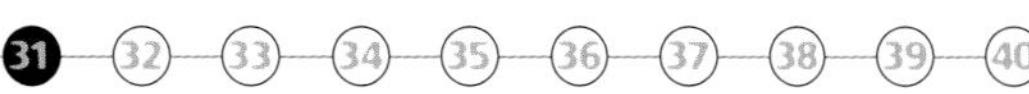

31

Taking Product Shots

Although product photography is mainly a commercial field, you do not need expensive equipment to take reasonably good shots. Whether you are a small business owner or an average consumer, you can use a digital camera to take pretty good shots of products.

Use Natural Light

It is important to avoid direct sunlight when taking product photos outdoors. The best times for a shoot are between 9 a.m. and 10 a.m. or 4 p.m. and 5 p.m.

When shooting indoors, place the product on a table next to the window so that it will be illuminated by a soft window light from the side. This technique gives excellent results. In fact, the play of shadow and light on the product can produce as good a result as any artificial studio lighting.

▲ A good use of natural light can give surprisingly good results.

Using a Background Sheet

If you have a messy background, cover it with a background sheet to create a simple background and keep the focus on the product. Even if you have an uncluttered background, you may wish to use a background sheet for its color and design to create an atmosphere that complements the product.

▲ The brown background sheet color-coordinates the products in this photo.

▲ A white sheet with patterns is used to emphasize the transparency of the tea set.

Use Household Lamps

Instead of using the camera's built-in flash, it is better to use an external light source, like a lamp. Although it won't be as bright as the flash, the light from the lamp can make the product look more natural and bring out the contours and texture of the product.

▲ Product photo taken without using a light source.

▲ Product photo taken using a lamp.

▲ You can use any lamp around the house.

Use a Tripod

When shooting product shots, you will spend most of your time changing the position of the product and the background elements to try out different compositions. To prevent fatigue, you should use a tripod. In addition, since neither household nor office lighting is as bright as studio lights, you will need a longer exposure time to take a product shot. As this increases the risk of camera shake and blurring, a tripod is absolutely necessary.

Increase the Exposure

Product photos need to be well lit and stand out from the background. If you use the Auto exposure specified by the camera, your photos will appear slightly dark. This is because the camera will average out the exposure for the scene to 18 percent gray. The solution is to override the Auto exposure and open up the aperture or slow down the shutter speed by 1 or 2 stops.

For cameras that have an exposure compensation feature, raise the exposure compensation by one or two levels before you take the photo. Alternatively, set the camera to the AEB, or Auto Exposure Bracketing mode. The camera will shoot at three different exposures in three continuous shots from which you can select the best photo.

▲ Using Auto exposure in direct light without exposure compensation will make the photo slightly dark.

▲ Exposure raised by 1 stop

▲ Exposure raised by 2 stops

▲ Use a piece of paper to reflect the light from a lamp.

▲ Raise the exposure by 2 stops when using reflected light.

 **Built-In Flash**

Do not use the camera's built-in flash when taking product photos, as this will create harsh shadows.

Use a Simple Still-Life Lighting Package

Shooting good product photos requires several large light sources and a background lamp. Such equipment is expensive and can be too bulky to store in regular households. For hobbyists, a simple still-life photography lighting package is a less expensive option and works just as well for small products and still-life setups.

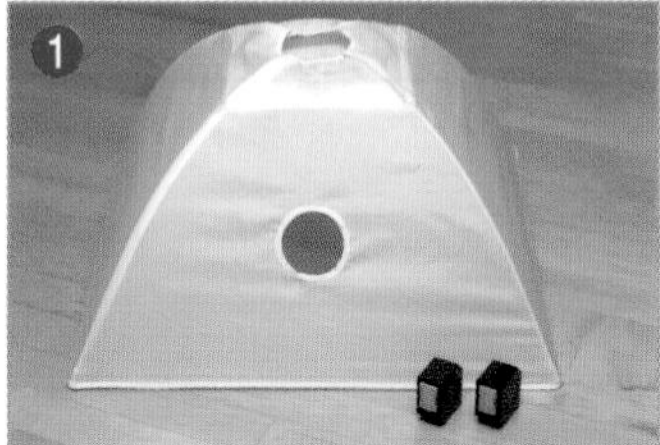

▲ The set includes two small lamps and a box for displaying the product.

▲ Place the background sheet on a flat surface, place the product on top, and position the lamps.

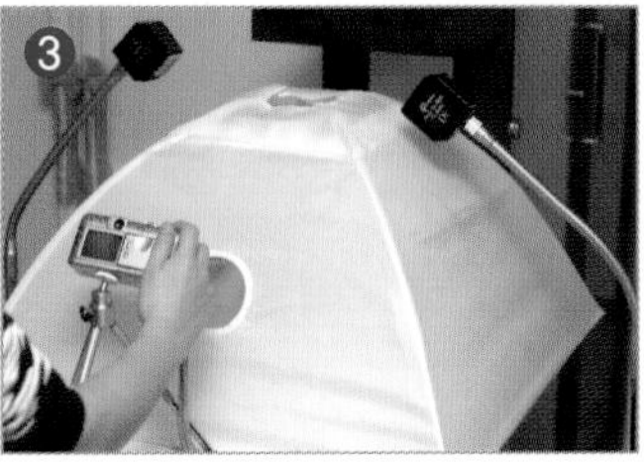

▲ After covering the diffusion box and setting up the camera, use the flash to take the photo. The two lamps will flash at the same time.

▲ No shadows will be cast on the white background.

▲ Even objects with highly reflective surfaces can be photographed in this way without any problems.

A typical lighting package includes two small lamps and a diffusion box to soften the light and eliminate harsh shadows. These lights are smaller, making them easier to set up and store, and they can also be triggered wirelessly, making them suitable for use with digital cameras.

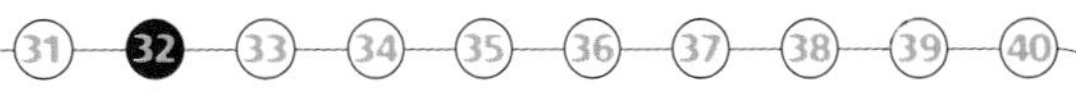

32

Taking Photos of Cars

Cars are not only modes of transportation designed to get you quickly from one place to another; they are also objects of beauty and precision engineering. While vacationing in another country, you will probably see many makes and models that are not found back home. If you love cars, try taking photos of them with your digital camera.

Shooting Close-Ups

Although full shots are great, you should also try to take photos of a car at different distances and perspectives to add variety to your selection of photos. Study the form of the car, pick out its most attractive features, and fill the frame with it. For example, you may want to shoot a close-up of a specific area in order to emphasize the beauty of the car's contours or the power of its build.

▶ Taking a close-up lets the viewer study the car's design elements in detail.

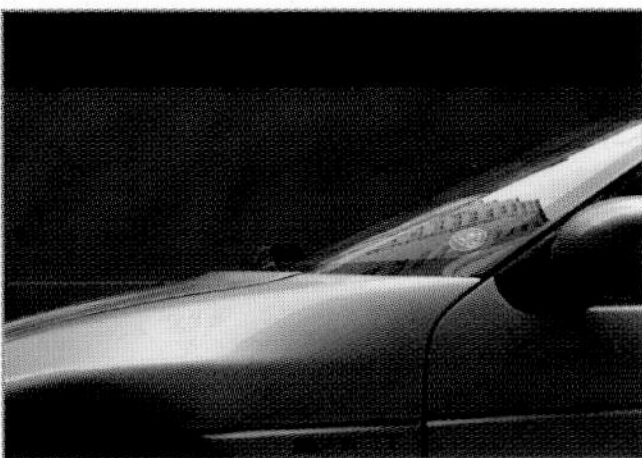

◀▲ Emphasizing the sleek contours

▲ Close-ups can turn images into an abstract study of form, color, and light.

▲ Emphasize the power of the car by taking a close-up shot of the engine.

Weather and Time of Day

The weather and time of day affects not only the exposure but also the color and the mood of your image.

▲ Turn on the headlights when shooting at sunset to capture the fleeting sensation of day turning into night.

▲ The rain makes the car and the road highly reflective, giving it a sleek appearance.

▲ The muted colors and foggy conditions at dawn provide a contrast and bring out the car in the image.

Lens Type

When taking photos of cars, use a wide-angle lens to deepen the depth of field and keep the background in focus. Including the background will make the image more interesting, as it says something about the car's owner and the neighborhood.

▲ Try taking a few compositions that include the background.

Camera Angle

Instead of taking a shot from the front, stand slightly to the side to add dimension and perspective to the photo. Try to find an interesting angle; stand, squat, or lie on your belly if you have to.

▲ Classic cars always make nice subjects for photos. So, if you come across one, reach for your digital camera and click away!

Shutter Speed

You can use either a fast shutter speed to freeze the motion of a car or a slow shutter speed to blur the traffic around it.

▲ Use a fast shutter speed (1/200 second) or the Sports Scene mode to freeze a moving car.

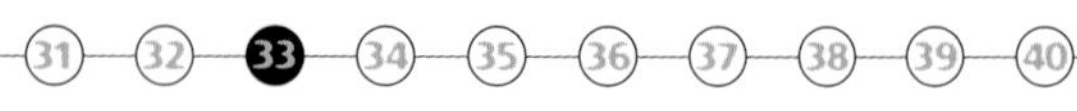

33 Shooting Architecture

When taking photos of building exteriors, you need to decide whether to include the entire building or just a section of it. The sheer size and height of some buildings makes it hard to include the entire structure without barrel distortion. However, by keeping a few things in mind, you can take spectacular photos of any structure, from your own house to massive architectural wonders.

Use a Telephoto Lens

Most people tend to leave too much space in their image by including too much of the background or the building. Remember that, while the wide expanse before you may look inspiring and majestic, the subjects will look insignificant and even diminutive when printed. If you are standing some distance away, you need to avoid shooting such broad, generalized views by using a telephoto lens to fill the frame with the subject. If you do not have a good telephoto lens, you should get closer to the building and photograph a major feature of the building.

▲ Fill the frame and you will start seeing a distinct improvement.

Introduce Foreground Objects

Where possible, include some meaningful objects or people in the foreground of your building shot to give it more depth, dimensionality, and thematic interest.

▲ A statue is included to give the photo a central focus.

▲ By introducing a soft element in the form of the flower bush, you can make a cold-looking apartment building appear more warm and welcoming.

Avoid Distortion

A wide-angle lens with a focal length of 35mm or less tends to create distortion at the photo edges and warp the straight edges of buildings The distortion gets more obvious with shorter focal lengths and taller buildings.

To snap a photo that will reproduce an image of the building without distortion, the lens must have a focal length of 50mm or more (telephoto). When shooting with a telephoto lens, a building can be captured as it is without any distortion but you will have to shoot from farther away to get more of the subject in the frame.

▲▶ Buildings can look distorted when shot with a wide-angle lens.

▲ Using a telephoto lens to shoot from a vantage point at a distance around half the height of the building will reduce distortion.

Vary the Composition

You can make your photo album livelier by using different compositions, angles, and props. Here are some ideas:

▲ Using leading lines and different camera angles creatively can produce many rewarding shots.

▲ When shooting at or from buildings, try using the doors, arches or windows to frame the subject.

▲ Shoot through a colored sheet with a hole or any other objects to selectively focus on the building.

▲ This image is kept simple by shooting only a small section of both buildings. The focus is on the form of the buildings rather than on the buildings per se.

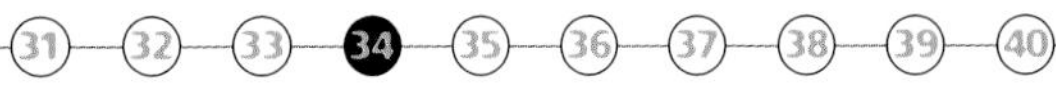

34

Taking Photos in a Museum or Art Gallery

Even if you are not a history buff or an avid art lover, you are likely to have visited museums or art galleries during your travels at one time or another.

While we will look at the techniques for taking photos at museums and art gallleries in this section, these same techniques can be applied in taking photos under other similar indoor conditions.

Glare and Reflection

Most displays in a museum are encased in glass, which can create reflections and glare in your photos if you use the flash. To overcome this problem, stand at a distance from the glass casing and shoot with a telephoto lens, without using a flash.

▲ You can't get a clear view of the display if you use a flash.

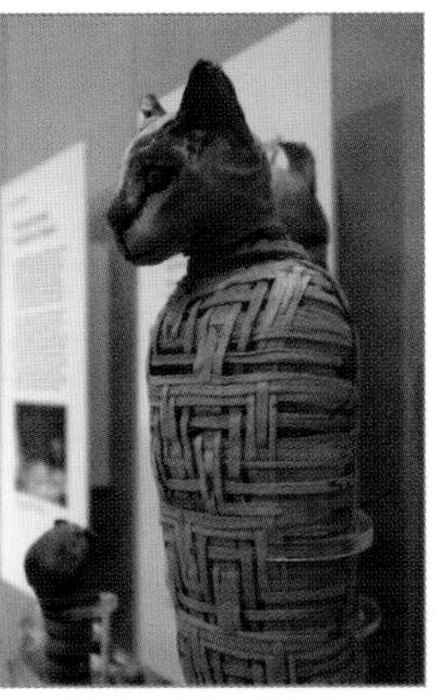

▲ Look for an angle with the least reflection.

Lighting

Since many museums are dimly lit indoor spaces, getting enough light for a good exposure becomes a problem. As most people set their cameras to Auto mode, the low-light conditions will trigger the flash. As you have just learned, this creates reflections in your image. To counteract this problem, deactivate the flash, set a slower shutter speed to let in more light, and hold the camera steady to prevent blurring. Another option is to take advantage of the natural light coming through the museum's windows.

▲ Take advantage of the natural light.

No Flash Photography

Many museums have strict regulations against photography because your camera's flash (together with the flash from millions of other tourists) can damage an artwork over a period of time. A way of getting the right exposure under these conditions is to increase the camera's sensitivity (ISO) to light.

▲ Photo taken at high sensitivity without using flash.

White Balance

Most museums use either incandescent or halogen lamps, which will cast an orange tint over your images. To avoid this, you must adjust the white balance to match the color temperature of the museum lights. Simply pick the Museum Scene mode or the Incandescent White Balance mode before taking photos.

▲ The colors are more accurate after you have adjusted the white balance.

Camera Distance

When photographing small displays, you should stand as close as you can to the glass case. For large sculptures, try to take close-up shots to eliminate the presence of other visitors and secondary objects from the background.

▲ You need to get really close to shoot small objects.

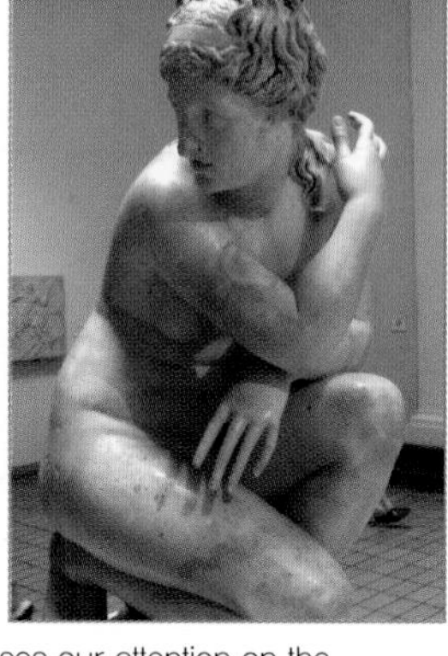

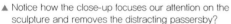

▲ Notice how the close-up focuses our attention on the sculpture and removes the distracting passersby?

▲ Take borderless, close-up shots of a mural or a drawing for a postcard look.

Museum Building

Many museums are housed in grand old buildings that are artworks in themselves. On your next trip to a museum, study the architecture and you will find many photo opportunities.

▲ The museum itself can be a work of art.

◀▲ You may also want to take a photo of the museum's exterior as a keepsake.

35

Photographing Pets

Pets are generally restless and move about constantly. Photographing pets can be tricky, because they won't pose for the camera and don't take instruction very well. Although it is difficult to take photos of pets, the results can be immensely satisfying. Another upside is that you get to combine two hobbies (i.e., photography and pets) into one.

Basic Techniques

▶▶▶ Use a Toy

Grab your pet's attention with its favorite toy or food. This will keep your pet amused long enough for you to take the photos.

▶▶▶ Avoid Flash

If you use a flash, the sudden burst of bright light can frighten your pet or make its eyes look red in the photo. To overcome this problem, try to avoid using flash where possible or, if you must, use the Red-Eye Reduction mode found in most digital cameras.

▶▶▶ ISO and Shutter Speed

By increasing the camera's sensitivity (higher ISO) or opening up the aperture, you can use a fast shutter speed to capture the movement of your pets. You can achieve the same result by using the Sports Scene mode.

▲ A dangling, jingling toy did the trick with these two.

▲ You will need fast reflexes as well as fast shutter speeds to shoot your pet in action.

Advanced Techniques

▶▶▶ Continuous Shots

You never know when your pet will assume the look or gesture you want to photograph. To be sure that you don't miss the magic moment, use the Continuous Shot feature to take several successive shots and then choose the best from the lot.

▲ For randomly moving objects like pets, it is advisable to use the Continuous Shot feature.

▶▶▶ Selective Focusing

Open up to the maximum aperture (or use the Portrait mode) and use the selective-focusing technique to blur the background and keep the focus on your pet.

▲ Selective focusing has the effect of making the background and your pet look soft and fuzzy.

▶▶▶ Close-Ups

Try taking close-ups to communicate a sense of intimacy and familiarity.

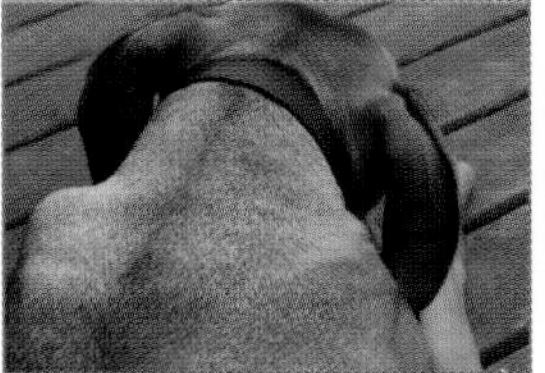

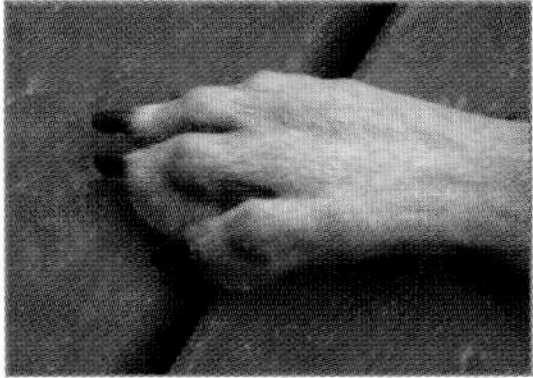

▲ You don't have to include your pet's face or its entire body in your photos. Try taking close-ups from a different angle or focus on a specific area.

▲ Use close-up shots to capture the cute expression on your pet's face.

▶▶▶ Experiment!

You can take photos of your pet in countless ways. To help you get started, here are a few ideas:

▲ Photograph your pet interacting with others to show its friendly nature.

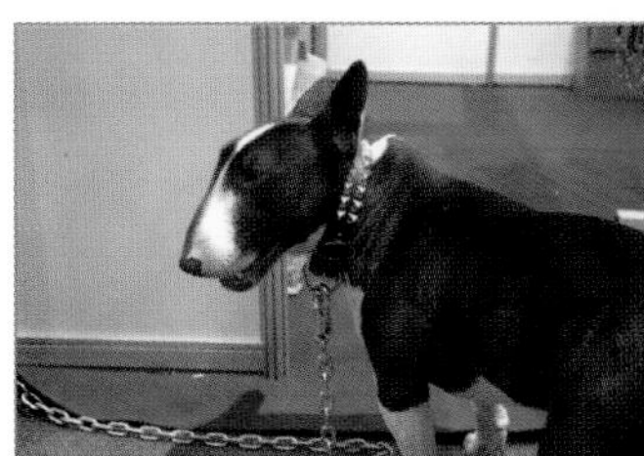

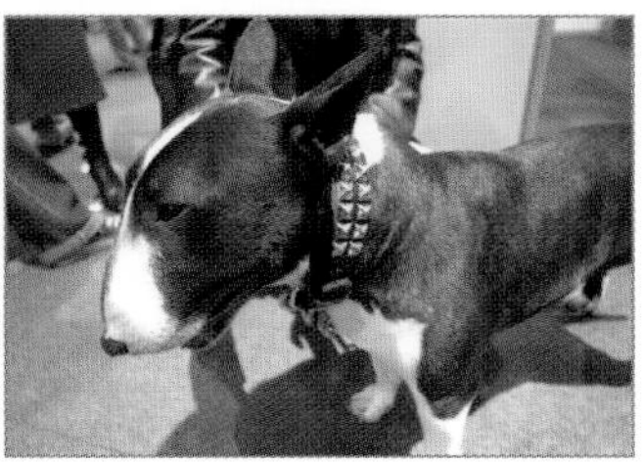

▲ Use a wide-angle lens (right) to take zany-looking shots of your pet.

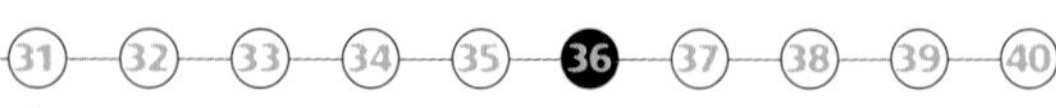

36 Shooting and Viewing Movies

Most digital cameras come with a Movie feature. Depending on your camera model, the Movie feature allows you to record movie clips of a few seconds or minutes in length. The movie clips are usually shot at a resolution of 320 x 240. Although the resolution is quite low, this feature is perfect for situations where photos alone are not quite enough for capturing the essence of the moment.

Recording a Movie on the Digital Camera

Shooting a short movie with your digital camera is really quite simple. First, select the Movie mode. Next, press the shutter-release button all the way down to start recording. Press the button again to stop.

Your movie will be stored in the Motion JPEG format, the QuickTime movie file format, or the Microsoft Windows Media Player format on your memory card. To find out which format your camera uses, you need to read your user manual.

▲ Changing to Movie mode

Voice Recording

Some digital cameras have a Voice Recording function that can record short voice messages. Again, read your user manual to see if your camera has this function.

Viewing Digital Images and Movies on TV

The Video-Out feature on your camera allows you to view the photos or movie clips you took on a TV screen. This feature is useful for showing your images or movies to a group of friends. In this way, they won't have to crowd around your camera or squint at the small LCD display.

To use the Video-Out feature, you need to connect one end of the AV cable supplied with your camera to the Video In port on the TV monitor and the other end to the Video/Audio Out port on the camera.

On most cameras, the AV cable port is located next to the USB port. The AV port allows you to output both sound and video from the camera. However, some cameras can only output video.

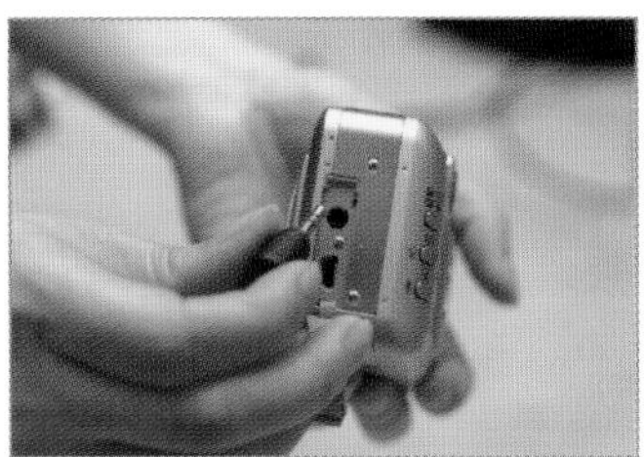

▲ Connecting the cable to the camera

Recording Digital Images and Movies Directly on the VCR

1. The Video-Out feature also allows you to use the digital camera like a camcorder. If you connect the AV cable to the Video/Audio In port of a VCR, you can record movie clips directly to videotapes rather than on the camera itself. The downside to this arrangement is that you can only record within the range of the setup.

◀ Connect the other end of the cable to the Video/Audio In port on the VCR.

2. Once the camera is connected to the VCR, you can connect the VCR to the TV to see what is being recorded.

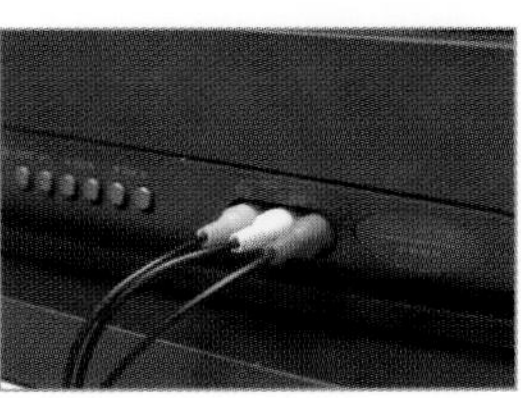

◀ Connecting the VCR and the TV.

③ Turn on the camera and switch to Movie mode. The scene on the LCD will also be displayed on the TV screen.

◀ The LCD view is displayed on the TV screen.

④ Press Record on the VCR to begin recording.

◀ Record the movie on the VCR.

Checklist

- When taking pictures of objects such as food and products, capture the defining characteristic, consider taking a close-up of part of the object, and use decorative elements and a background sheet if necessary.
- Spray water (fruits) or lightly glaze a food item (cooked dishes) with oil to make it look more appetizing.
- Try taking shots by the window for a soft lighting effect.
- Use household lamps instead of the flash for a more natural lighting effect. If the light from the lamp is too harsh, bounce it off a piece of white paper.
- When taking product shots, use a tripod as you will need to adjust the subject placement often.
- Use a still-life lighting package if you often take product shots.
- Use a telephoto lens to shoot architecture from a distance at around half the height of the building if you want to avoid distortion at the edges.
- In a museum or art gallery, shoot at an angle without using flash if shooting through glass, increase the sensitivity if there is no other way to properly expose the image, adjust the white balance, and shoot close-ups to exclude other tourists from the shot.
- When taking pictures of pets, use a toy; or turn off the flash and use a fast shutter speed, the Sports Scene mode or the Continuous Shot function.
- Use the Video-Out feature to show your photos or movie clips to a group of friends.

40 Digital Photography Techniques

Chapter 6

After the Photo Shoot

In this last chapter, you will learn how to connect, transfer, manage, and store the images taken with your digital camera on the computer. We will also look at some common options for printing your shots, explore the problem of color matching across devices, and discuss the appropriate image resolutions for your print size. In the last technique, you will learn how to use Photoshop Album to create your own photo gallery for the Internet.

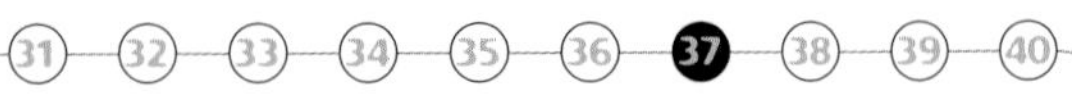

37

Connecting and Transferring Images to the Computer

If your camera uses CompactFlash, Memory Stick, SmartMedia, or any other removable storage media, you can pop it out from your camera and use a card reader or adapter connected to your computer to transfer the files. Alternatively, you can transfer images by linking your camera to your computer using a serial cable or USB cable. Yet another transfer method is through infrared. But since most new digital cameras use USB, we will only focus on this transfer method in this section.

Installing a Device Driver

Before you transfer images using a USB (Universal Serial Bus) cable, you need to install the camera's device driver on your computer. A device driver is software that enables a computer to communicate with other devices. The device driver for your digital camera usually comes with it on a diskette or CD-ROM. If your PC runs on Windows 98, the device driver needs to be installed manually. See the steps below.

1. Insert the Device Driver CD-ROM into the CD-ROM drive. An installation program will load automatically. Select [USB Driver for Windows 98] from the menu.

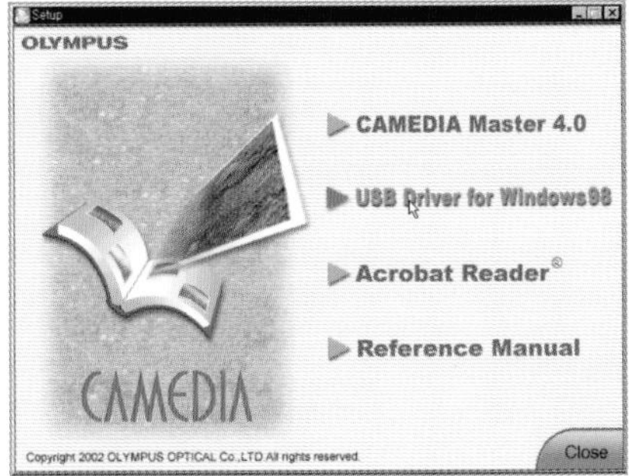

tip For PCs running Windows 2000/ME/XP, the installation is done automatically.

2 A dialog box will appear. Click Continue to start the installation process. Most installers require you to restart your computer before completing the installation process. After the computer is restarted, connect the camera to the computer and the installation will complete automatically. Read your camera's manual for more information on the installation of your device driver.

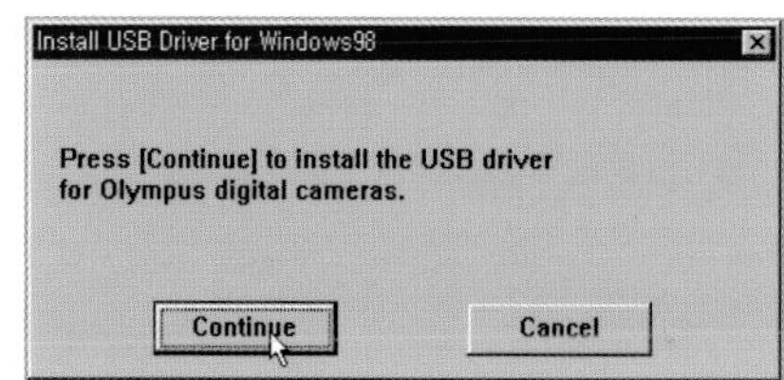

Connecting the Digital Camera to a Computer

1 Plug the flat connector of the USB cable into the computer's USB port, as shown.

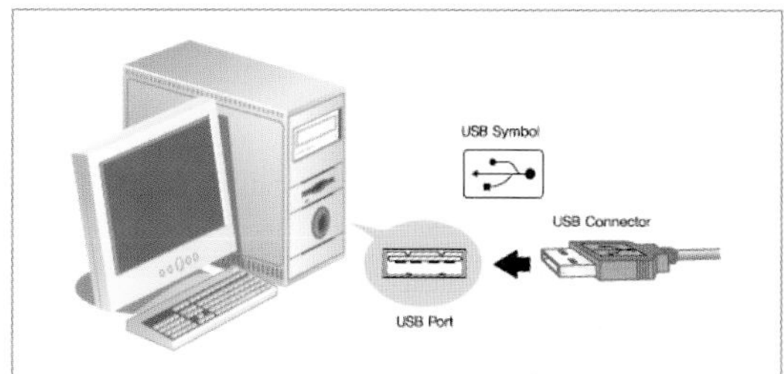

2 Flip the camera's USB connector cover open and plug the square end of the USB cable into the camera's USB connector, as shown. Keep the camera lens cover on at all times.

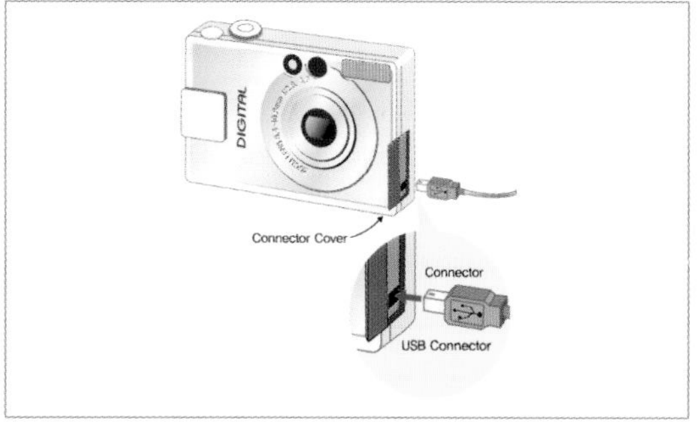

(3) If the device driver is installed, the following dialog box will appear automatically. You can transfer images to the computer by using the Scanner and Camera Wizard.

Using Dedicated Software Programs to Transfer Images

Some digital cameras require the use of dedicated software programs to transfer and manage images. For such cameras, you need to install the program before connecting them to the computer. As the steps vary from camera to camera, read the camera's manual for more information.

tip Use a Reliable Power Source

Before transferring data to the computer, make sure your camera's battery is fully charged.

Transferring Images to a Computer

The Scanner and Camera Wizard is a program that comes with your Windows operating system. It helps you transfer data from scanners and digital cameras to your computer. Once the camera is plugged into the computer, the wizard will recognize the digital camera as a removable storage media. The digital camera will then appear as an icon on the Scanners and Cameras window. You should activate Windows Explorer and start transferring the images to the computer. Once transferred, you can copy, move, rename, and erase the images through Windows Explorer. The folllowing steps show you where to locate the transferred images:

(1) Run Windows Explorer and click on [Removable Disk].

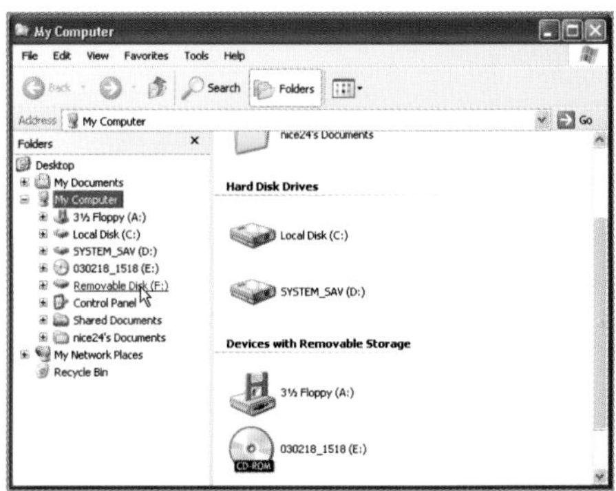

② A list of images stored in the camera's portable memory disk will be displayed. You can use Windows Explorer to manage the image files in the same manner as you would any other files on your computer.

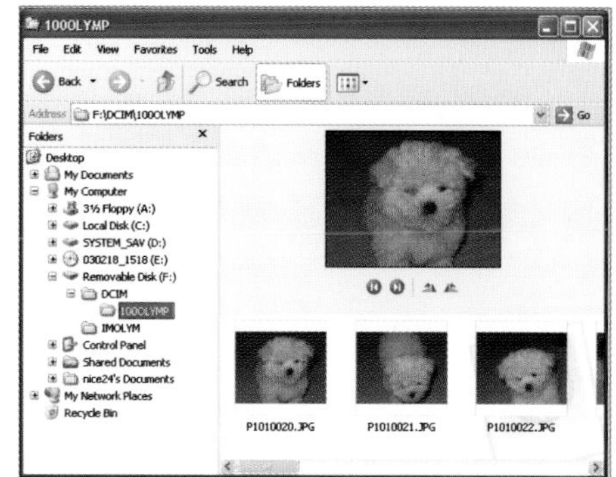

Special Directory for Images

Some cameras will save the images into a special directory. If such is the case, click on the folder where the images are stored to view the files. Read your camera's manual to final out about the special directories that images are automatically saved to.

Detaching a Camera from a PC

Once the images have been transferred, you have to disconnect the camera from the PC safely. Here's how:

▶▶▶ Windows 98 Users

① Right-click on [Removable Disk] in the My Computer window and choose [Eject].

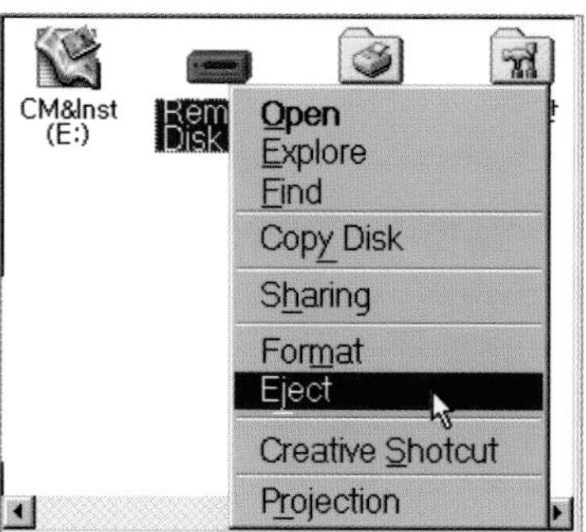

② The light, which shines green to indicate that the camera is connected to a PC, will turn off. Disconnect the cable from the camera and the computer.

▶▶▶ Windows 2000/ME/XP Users

① Click on [Safely Remove Hardware] from the taskbar and choose [Safely Remove USB Mass Storage Device-Drive].

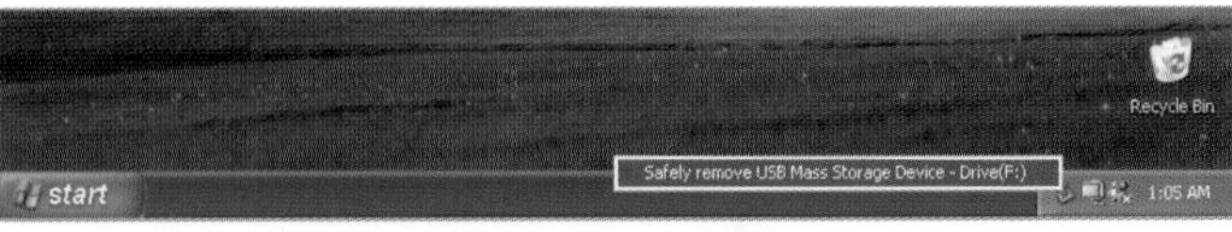

② When the Safely Remove Hardware dialog box appears, click on the [Stop] button. Disconnect the cable from the camera and PC after the Safe to Remove Hardware message is displayed.

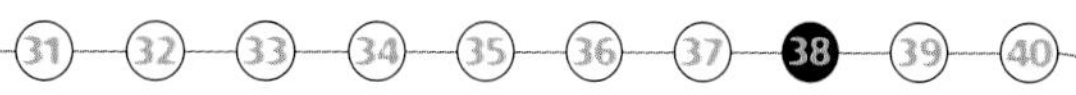

38 Organizing and Managing Images

The best part of owning a digital camera is that you can take as many photos as you want without worrying about the additional expense of film and developing fees. Ironically, this can be too much of a good thing. With a large library of images, you may end up searching your hard disk for the image you want in vain. To avoid this nightmare, it is important that you organize and manage your images well.

Renaming Images One at a Time

A digital camera automatically assigns the images you take with file names like DSCN0030.jpg. As you can see, the names are meaningless and do not describe the images at all. This becomes a problem when you have to look for a particular image from the tens or hundreds that you have shot. To make it easier to identify the images, you should rename the images in a way that is meaningful to you. Let's see how you can do this:

1. First, transfer the images to your computer. Select the images you want to keep and delete the rest.

2. Rename the selected images. For example, I named the temple shot I took on a trip to Japan in 2003 as japan-2003-kyoto-temple1.jpg. The file name should get more descriptive toward the end. If I had named my shot as temple1-kyoto-2003-japan.jpg, my shots would have been listed by the generic "temple" first and the more specific location, "kyoto," second.

3. Save the images in a folder named in the same descriptive way. You may want to keep notes or other information about the images that you take in the same folder.

4. Back up your images on CD-ROMs. Label the CD-ROMs. For example, Japan 2003 Photo CD 6.

Using ACDSee

There are many programs designed to help you manage and edit your photos. In this section, we will look at ACDSee, a popular digital camera program for PCs. The main advantage of ACDSee is its easy-to-use image viewer. It allows users to view images in three different ways: Folder Tree, Thumbnail, and Preview.

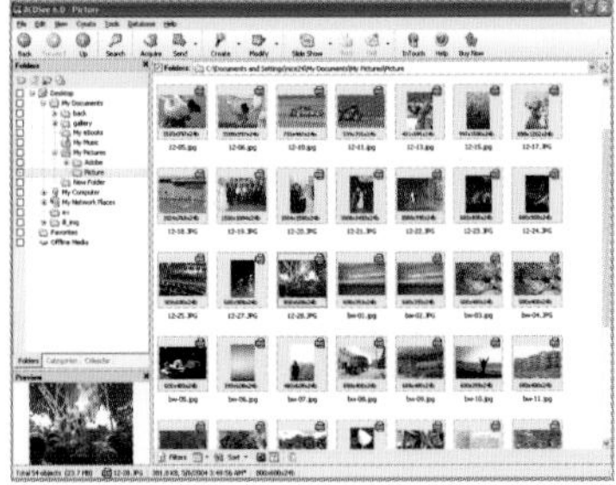

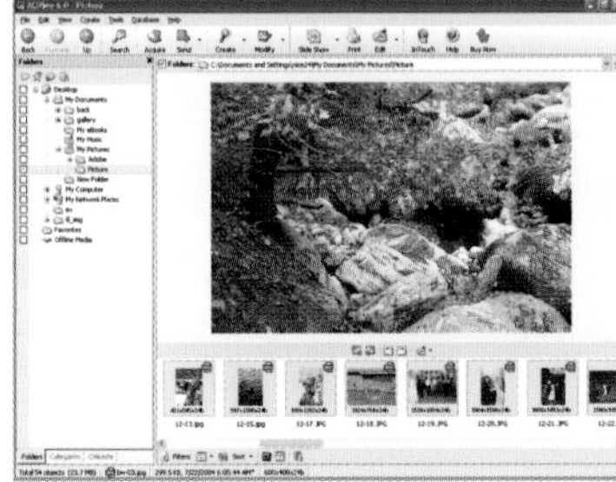

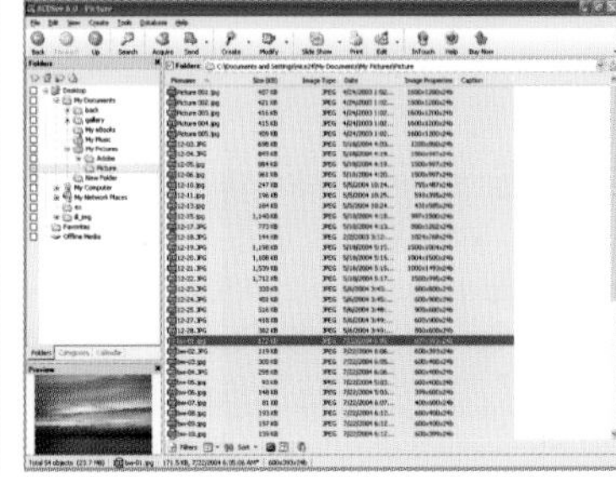

▲ User-friendly Thumbnail and Preview functions

▶▶▶ The menu at the top consists of the following options:

- Acquire: Imports images from a digital camera or scanner.

▲ Imports images when Acquire icon is clicked.

- Edit: You can choose to edit in ACDSee or Foto Canvas from the menu in version 6.0.

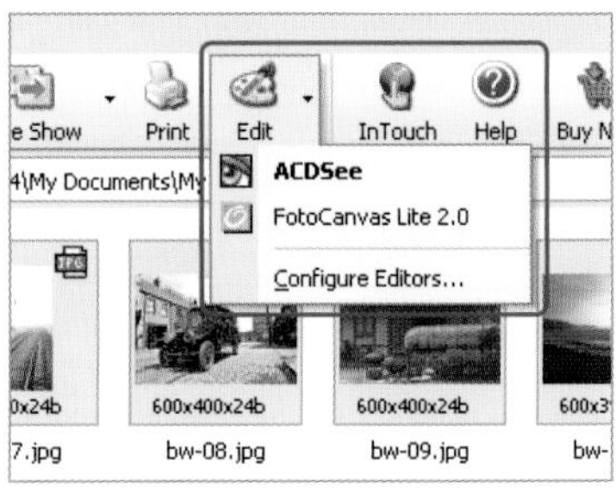

▲ Click [Edit] to touchup and enhance your images.

- Create: Create a slide show, compact disc, or other HTML documents.

▶ You can do many fanciful things with the Create function.

▶▶▶ Properties

Displays information about an image.

Information about an image, which may be useful for future reference, is stored in the [Metadata] tab.

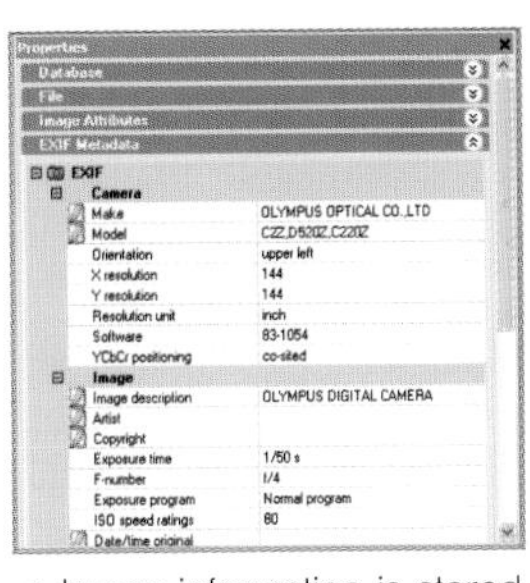

▲ Image information is stored in the [Metadata] tab.

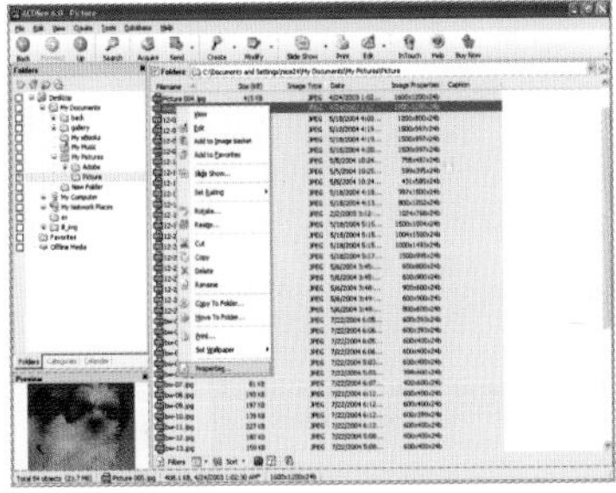

▲ Select an image, right-click, and choose [Properties].

▶▶▶ Batch Rename

Use the [Batch Rename] tool to rename a batch of images at the same time.

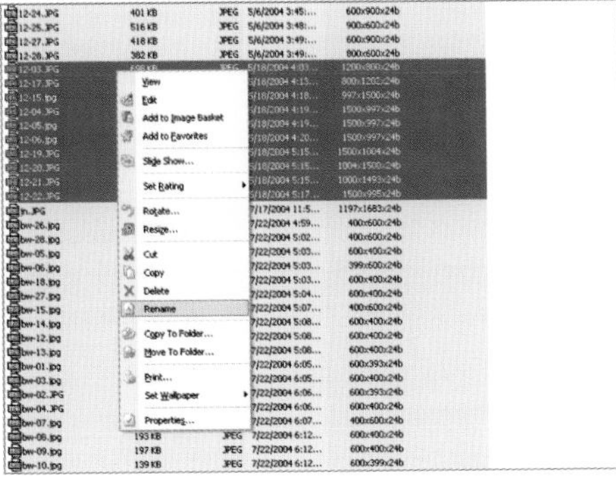

▲ Select the images and right-click [Rename].

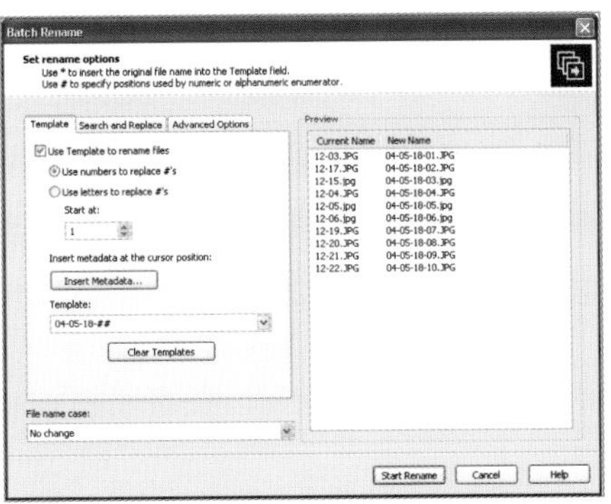

▲ With the wildcard function, ###, numbers in running order are applied automatically to the selected images.

▶▶▶ Image Rotate

Vertical images can be easily rotated with the [Image Rotate] function.

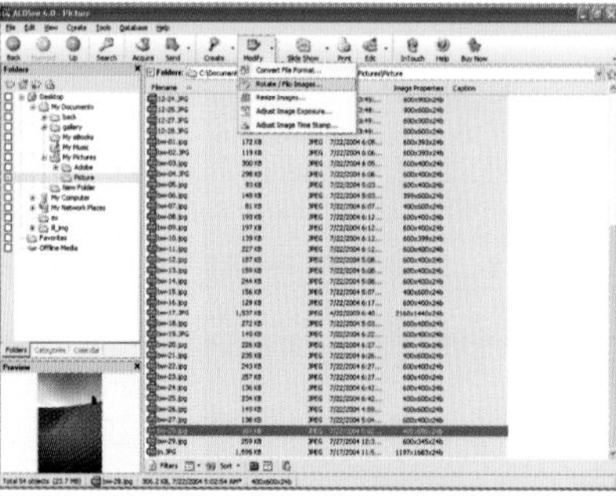

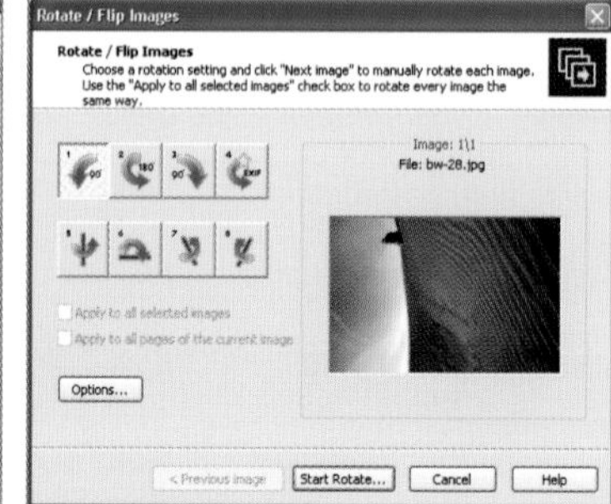

▲ Using the [Image Rotate] function

▶▶▶ Resize

You can adjust the size and resolution of an image using the [Resize] function in the menu.

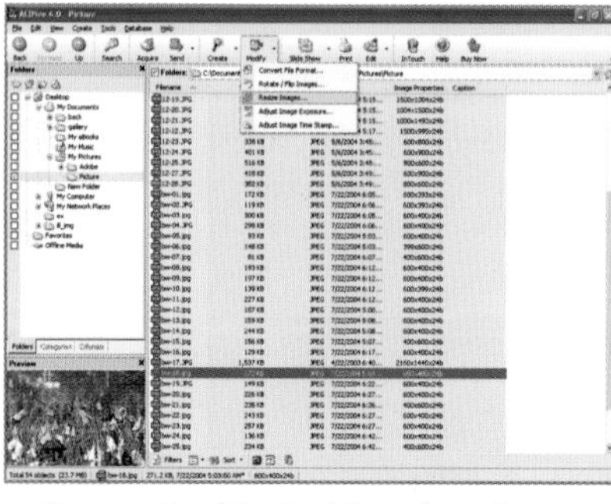

▲ Choose the [Resize] icon from the menu.

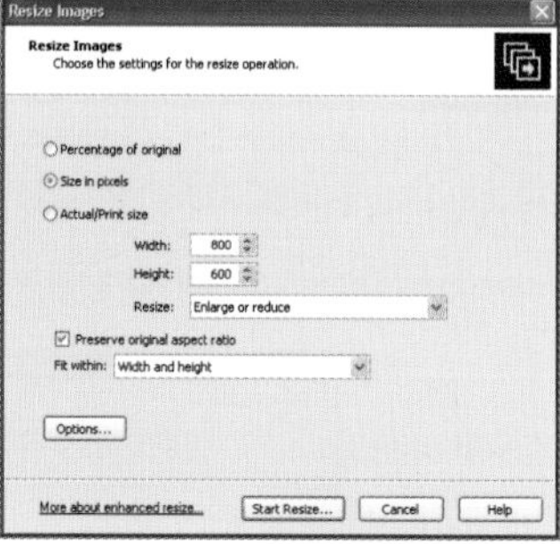

▲ Change the image resolution.

39 Developing Photos

A big advantage of digital images over film cameras is that you can choose to print only the images you want and do it right at home. In fact, you can print anywhere if you own one of those small portable photo printers meant for people on the move. As image-editing software, consumer photo printers, and paper become better and more affordable, it has become possible for average consumers to produce high-quality prints that match those from a photofinisher.

Printing at Home

▶▶▶ Using a General Document Printer

You can use normal 8 ½ x 11 inch paper or photo paper specially made for printing photographs. Although photo paper is expensive, you can produce quality prints on it that come close to the quality of normal photographs. When using a general printer, you can use image-editing programs such as Windows XP's Photo Printing Wizard or Adobe's Photoshop to print.

Editing the Image

Before you print, you can use the Foto Canvas Program to perform simple image-editing operations.

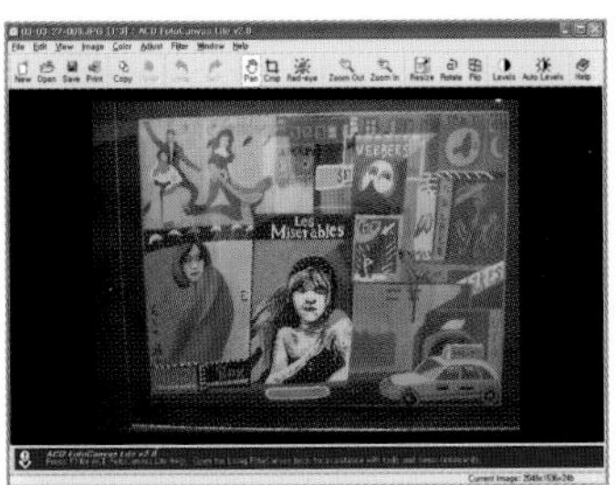

▲ Running Foto Canvas

▲ Click the [Levels] icon to do simple image-editing operations.

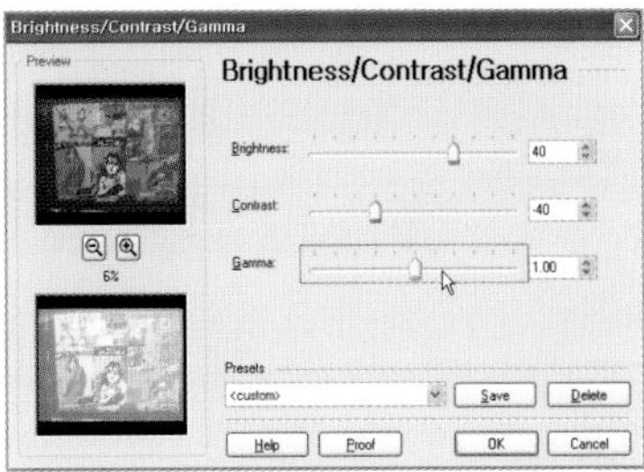

▲ You can do detail adjustments for brightness and contrast.

●Using Photo Printing Wizard to Print

① Select an image, right-click, and choose [Print].

② Photo Printing Wizard will begin.

If you are not selecting any special options, keep clicking on [Next] until you reach the layout option screen. Choose a layout and click on [Next]. Your photo will start printing soon.

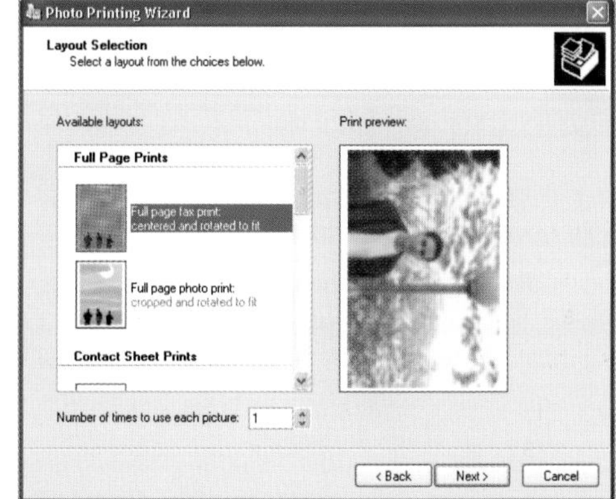

●Using Photoshop Elements to Print

Before you start printing, you have to set an output resolution. Generally images used for the Web have a resolution of 72 dpi. However, to get a reasonably good print on photographic paper, the images should have a resolution of 200 to 300 dpi.

▶▶▶ Using a Photo Printer

When using photo printers, you do not need a computer to print, which makes the process a lot simpler. You can print photos by simply inserting your camera's memory card into the photo printer. These days, even low-priced photo printers in the market will give you good value for money in terms of cost and performance, so shop around if you intend to buy a photo printer. Read your printer's manual to learn more about the printing process.

▲ Canon's photo printer

Calibrating the Monitor and the Printer

Monitors display colors on the screen by using a mix of red, green, and blue (RGB) lights while printers print colors in a mix of cyan, magenta, yellow, and black (CMYK) inks. Due to the difference in the way that color is recorded and output from these devices, the range of colors produced by both color models do not correspond accurately to each other or overlap completely.

So, if you notice that the colors in your image look significantly different when printed, you may need to match the colors on your monitor to your printer. This process of matching color across devices is called calibration. You can calibrate your devices using a color matching software, but this requires patience and experimentation or you may end up with worse prints than before.

Alternatively, you can look at the printed copy and try to change the colors on the monitor for a more accurate print. But this means that your image will print differently on another printer. Before you calibrate your devices, check to see if the color difference is due to the paper quality, ink purity, or the lighting conditions. It is easier to fix these problems than to calibrate colors.

Sending Prints to Professional Printers

Even though you can print your images at home, you may still want to send your non-urgent prints to a photofinisher for a couple of reasons. For instance, if you want to print hundreds of shots, you may find that it takes too much time and effort to print them at home. You can also get better and larger prints at a photofinisher, as they have more sophisticated equipment and they can also correct the color of your images. At these photofinishers, you can print high-quality photos and enlargements of more than 10 x 15 inches in size. For the best prints, make sure that you discuss your need with the printer and are specific about the results you want.

Another option is to use a web-based print service, but you will need to register as a member first. Online providers usually provide 50MB to 100MB of storage space for each account. Customers have to upload the images and specify sizes when they place an order. The provider then prints the photos and delivers them by post or express delivery in about three to five days. The cost is about the same as printing from film negatives. An added benefit is that you can also use the allocated storage space as your own image archive to share your photos with friends.

Additional options include printing your images at Fuji Film's FDI Stations if they are found in your neighborhood or at general photo studios, which are beginning to offer such services as well.

Adjusting the Aspect Ratio

Most images shot by digital cameras have an aspect ratio of 4:3, although some have a ratio of 3:2. Aspect ratio refers to the ratio of the image's height and width. However, the aspect ratio of most prints is different from the images' aspect ratio. Prints usually come in the ratio of 3:5, 4:6, 5:7, 8:10, 11:14, or 10:15.

So, if an image with an aspect ratio of 3:2 is printed on a photographic paper with an aspect ratio of 10:8, part of the image will be cut off. Since 3:2 = 12:8, the image will be cut off lengthwise on one or both sides.

▲ Original image with a ratio of 3:2

▲ Photo gets cut off when printed on 8 X 10 inch photographic paper

▶▶▶ Full Image Option

A way to prevent your images from being cut off is to order your prints in Full Image option. This option preserves the image ratio but leaves a margin on both sides of the photo. The actual size of the photo may shrink a little.

▲ Original image with a ratio of 3:2

▲ Printed in Full Image option on 8 X 10 inch paper.

▶▶▶ Photoshop Element's Crop Function

You can use the crop function in Photoshop to crop the image so that it will fit on 8 × 10 inch paper when printed. This method is recommended because you can crop the image according to your own preference and resize the image to fit the print size. Some printers support a Trim and Print service where users can crop their own images before printing.

▲ Original image with a ratio of 3:2

▲ Printed image after being cropped to fit a ratio of 8:10.

Recommended Resolutions

To get a good-quality print at a certain size, you should make sure that your original image resolution is high enough for that particular print size.

Paper Size (Inches)	Recommended (Minimun) Resolution	Number of Pixels on Digital Camera
3 x 5	1024 x 768	850,000
4 x 6	1280 x 1024	1,400,000
5 x 7	1600 x 1200	2,100,000
8 x 10	2048 x 1536	3,340,000
11 x 14	2272 x 1704	4,130,000

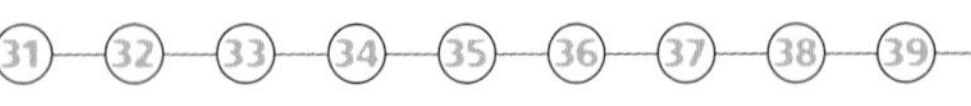

40

Setting Up Your Own Photo Gallery

With film cameras, you have to print and then scan your images into the computer before you can share them on the Internet. If you have scanned images before, you know what a hassle it can be. You need to correct the colors, align the photo, wait for it to scan, remove artifacts, and so on. With digital cameras, you can share your images very easily. In this section, we will look at how you can use Adobe Photoshop Album to create a photo gallery of your digital images for the Web.

Understanding the Menu Bar

Adobe Photoshop Album lets you organize and share your images very easily. With the software, you can fix common photo problems, assemble slideshows and put your images into cards, calendars, and more. Let's have a look at the options on the menu bar:

▶▶▶ File Menu

Lets you import digital images from devices such as scanners, digital cameras, or external storage media, and carry out functions such as creating back-up files or printing.

File Edit View Tag Find Creations Onl

Get Photos	▸
Catalog...	Ctrl+Shift+C
Archive...	
Backup...	
Restore...	
Reconnect All Missing Files...	
Rename...	
Export...	Ctrl+E
Attach to E-mail...	
Page Setup...	Ctrl+Shift+P
Print...	Ctrl+P
Exit	Ctrl+Q

▶▶▶ Edit Menu

Lets you do editing jobs such as copying or rotating images and creating wallpapers or captions for the images.

Edit View Tag Find Creations Online Serv

Undo Import Items	Ctrl+Z
Redo	Ctrl+Y
Copy	Ctrl+C
Select All	Ctrl+A
Select None	Ctrl+Shift+A
Add to Workspace	Ctrl+Shift+V
Fix Photo...	
Edit with Photoshop Elements...	
Cancel External Edit	
Rotate Right	Ctrl+R
Rotate Left	Ctrl+Shift+R
Adjust Date and Time...	
Revert to Original	
Replace Original with Edited	
Duplicate Item	
Clear Caption	
Update Thumbnail	
Reconnect Missing File...	
Delete from Catalog...	Del
Set as Desktop Wallpaper	
Preferences...	Ctrl+K

▶▶▶ View Menu

Lets you view the images through a variety of methods like a slideshow, full screen mode, and other viewing formats.

View Tag Find Creations Online Serv

	Slideshow	Ctrl+Space
	Show Full Screen	F11
	Refresh	F5
	Go To	▸
	Size	▸
	Arrangement	▸
	Media Types...	
✔	Show Dates and Tags	Ctrl+D
	Contact Book...	Ctrl+Alt+B
✔	Timeline	Ctrl+L
	Tags	Ctrl+T
	Properties	Alt+Enter
	Workspace	Ctrl+W
	Calendar	Ctrl+Alt+C

▶▶▶ Creation Menu

Lets you create electronic photo albums, slideshows, video CDs, and other viewing options.

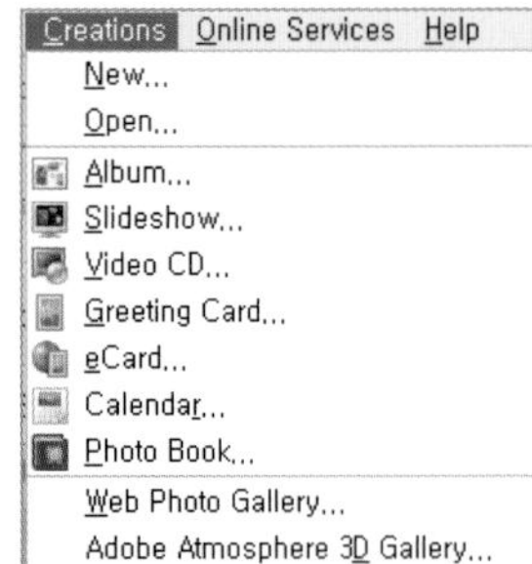

Fast Guide: Creating a Web Photo Gallery

① Go to [Files]-[Get Photos] to import the images from your hard disk or digital camera.

② After selecting all your images for your gallery, click on [Creations]-[Web Photo Gallery].

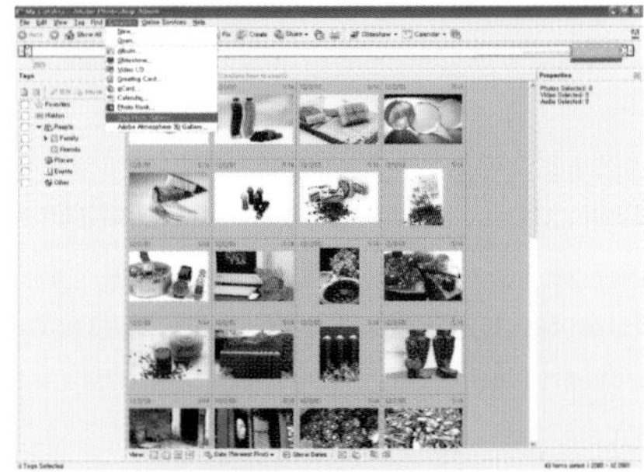

③ Choose a style for your photo gallery from the Gallery Style option. On the right side of the screen, you can preview the style of your gallery.

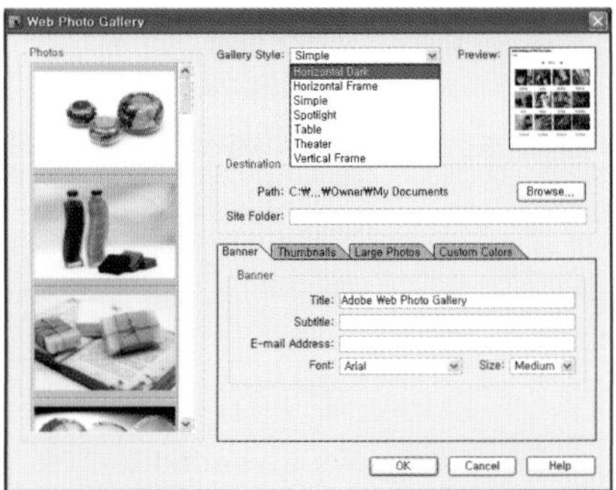

④ After assigning a Site Folder, choose the image's size and caption-related options. Then click Ok to start the photo gallery creation process. Here, we have chosen Large Photos for the image size.

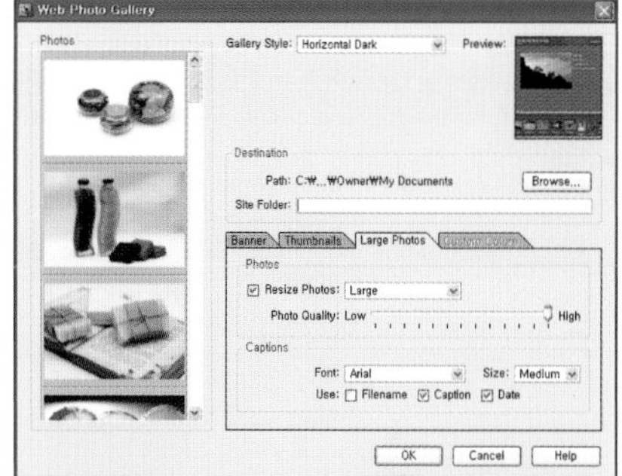

⑤ When your gallery is completed, a Web Photo Gallery Browser will appear, as shown.

⑥ If you run Windows Explorer and go to the previously set Site Folder, you will find many folders and the index.html file created in that directory. Double-click on this index file and your web browser will appear and display your gallery as in the example shown.

⑦ Once you have uploaded the Site Folder onto a server or website, your friends can view your photo gallery over the Internet.

- Install a device driver, if you have't already done so.
- Connect your camera to the computer and transfer your images using the Scanner and Camera Wizard program in the Windows operating system.
- Use ACDSee or other similar programs to manage and edit your images.
- Use ACDSee or other similar programs to rename your images in batches.
- Print your images using a general document printer at home, send them to a photofinisher, or upload them to a web-based print service.
- Set up your own photo gallery with Adobe Photoshop Album or other similar programs.
- Make CD covers using the coverXP freeware or create screen savers using the Screen Saver Builder shareware found in this book's supplementary CD.
- If you are interested in editing your images, you may wish to check out our book, *40 Digital Photo Retouching Techniques.*

Feature | Camera Phones

In the last year or so, the availability of camera phones at affordable prices has stirred up a storm of cell phone upgrades the world over. And as camera phones become increasingly popular, many people are now taking pictures using their camera phones. In this feature, we will look at the camera function found in cell phones and the techniques for taking pictures with camera phones. Because affordable camera phone models generally have extremely basic camera functions, we will also look at the camera functions found in top-of-the-line models.

Camera Function in Phones

In this section, we will look at the features that are important to taking pictures with a camera phone. Because new phone models are launched every so often, this section also covers the latest camera phone developments in Korea and Japan to keep the information in this section relevant for some time. The phones found in Korea and Japan are typically more advanced than the ones found in the rest of the world.

▶▶▶ Resolution

Most phones that are on the market now have a resolution between 100,000 pixels and 300,000 pixels. In some product brochures or other marketing materials, you may see the words CIF or VGA. This is another way of indicating the resolution of the camera's semiconductor. CIF refers to a resolution of 352 × 288 = 101,376 pixels, while VGA refers to 640 × 480= 307,200 pixels. As you might have noticed, this is much lower than the 3 megapixels (3,000,000 pixels) resolution that you can expect from today's automatic digital cameras.

With a resolution that is less than 2 megapixels, pictures taken using camera phones cannot print up to 4R. Given the speed at which new camera models and technologies emerge, however, this will not be a problem for long. In Korea and Japan, 1- to 2-megapixel phones are already the norm, and it is likely that you can expect camera phones with 3 megapixels in the near future. Samsung, for instance, launched a 3.2-megapixel camera phone in Korea in July 2004.

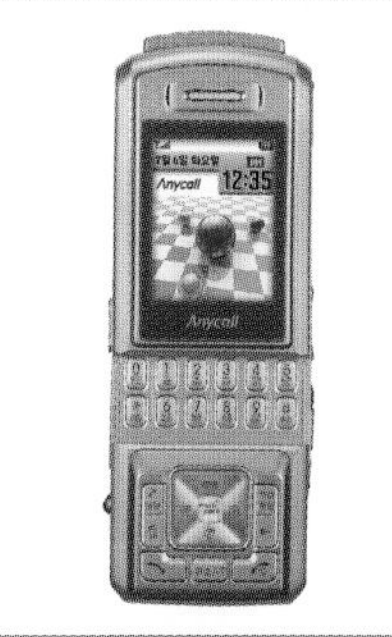

▲ Anycall SPH2300: Samsung's 3.2-megapixel Camera Phone with three times optical zoom

▶▶▶ Image Resolution and Quality

If a camera phone has a small storage capacity, you can lower the resolution and quality at which to capture the image. As you may know, the choice of resolution can only go as high as the resolution of the camera phone. On some phones, you can also set the image quality, which determines how much an image is compressed.

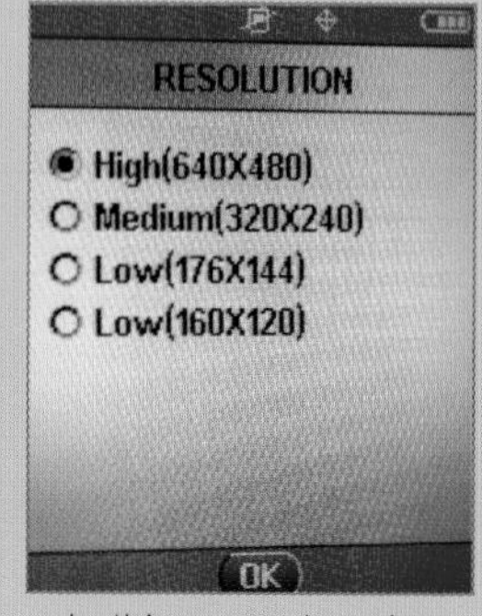

▲ In this example using a 300,000 pixel phone, there are four image sizes available.

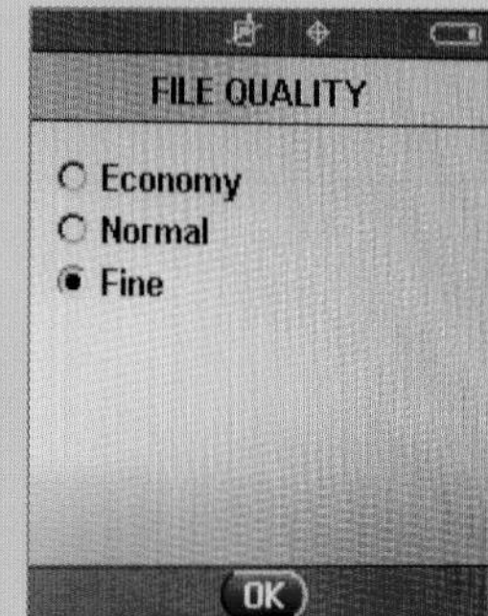

▲ Select the Fine option to use a low rate of compression.

▶▶▶ Display

The LCD on most camera phones can display 65,000 colors or more, while the best ones can display around 260,000 colors. If a phone's LCD screen displays only 4096 colors, you may see color banding on the screen. In addition, you may notice that images look sharper on the computer screen than on the phone's screen. This will happen if images are displayed on the camera's LCD at a resolution that is lower than the resolution that they are recorded and then shown on computer.

The color display and size of the LCD is important, because pictures taken using camera phones are frequently used as screen wallpaper, photo-caller ID, or shown on-screen to others. Another important factor is whether the LCD uses active TFT or passive STN display. An active TFT display is better than a passive STN display. With a passive STN display, the image on the LCD can be difficult to see when you are under bright sunlight.

For digital cameras, the LCD screen is expected to have a 65,000-color TFT display at the minimum, so the topic of LCD screen quality is a non-issue and you may not even find any information about a digital camera's LCD screen in the product specifications.

▶▶▶ Lens

All the camera phones in the market use lenses with a fixed focal length. This means that the zoom capability stated in camera phone specifications refers to digital zoom and not optical zoom. Generally speaking, you can expect to find 4X or 5X digital zoom in the new, higher-end camera phone models. In Japan and Korea, however, the latest camera phones are equipped with 3X optical zoom or have converter lenses that you can attach to change the built-in lenses' focal length. These developments are rapidly closing the gap between camera phones and digital compact.

Presently, it is not possible to set the shutter speed or aperture using camera phones, and this limits the kind of photos that you can take with camera phones. In the future, camera phones will certainly take on all the features of automatic digital compacts. It is just a matter of time. In Korea and Japan, we are already seeing the encroachment of camera phones into the lower end of the digital photography market even as digital camera makers move up-market.

▲ Converter lens for camera phones.

▲ Attaching a converter lens to a camera phone.

▶▶▶ Rotating Lens or LCD

Some camera phones have a rotating lens or LCD, while others have a small reflective mirror. These features are very popular because they make it easy for users to take self-portraits.

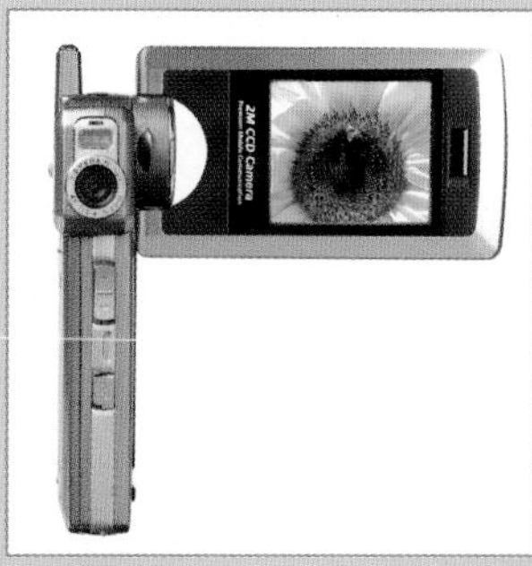

▲ A camera phone with a rotating LCD.

▶▶▶ Brightness and ISO

On some phones you will find the Brightness function, which lets you adjust the brightness of the image. In Korea and Japan, the phones also come with an ISO function that ranges from ISO 100 up to ISO 1600.

▲ Changing the ISO setting from ISO 100 to ISO 1600 brightens up the image considerably.

▶▶▶ Flash

Most camera phones do not have a flash, and those that do have a weak LED flash that is only useful if your subject is really close. But this is also changing of course. The latest models in Korea and Japan are equipped with a camera flash with adjustable brightness.

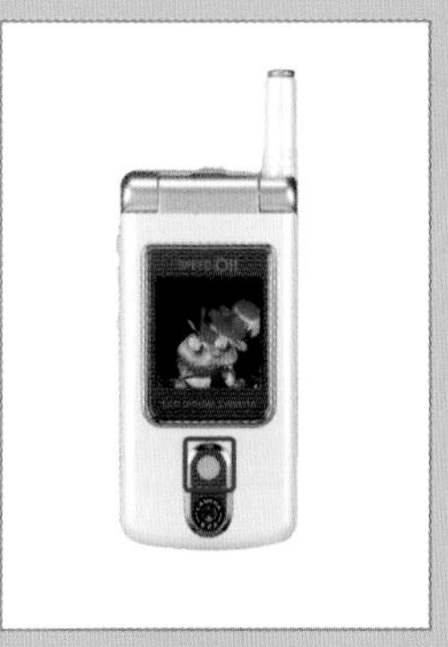

▲ A camera phone with a built-in LED flash.

▶▶▶ White Balance

Some camera phones are equipped with the White Balance function. Most camera phones have only a few white balance options (Automatic, Indoor, Outdoor), while the latest phones in Korea and Japan let the user set white balance manually and contain more white balance options.

▲ Try out different White Balance modes to remove a color cast.

▶▶▶ Image Editing

Many new high-end camera phones contain simple image-editing functions that let you create fun images that you can use as wallpaper or caller photo-ID or share with friends. You can insert text, frames, icons, or images to embellish the picture you took or apply an effect to change it completely. Some examples are the Black and White, Mosaic Blur, and Distort effects. In addition, you can perform simple editing such as rotate, flip, scale, and move.

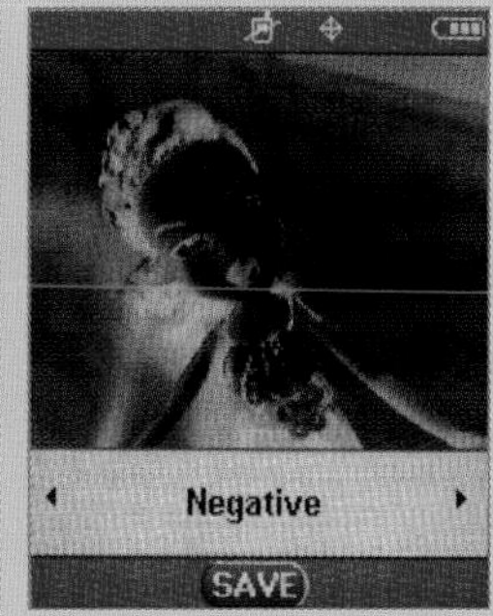

▲ Applying the Antique (left) and Negative (right) effect on an image

▶▶▶ Self-Timer

When taking group shots, it can be useful to have the Self-Timer function which lets you place the camera farther away than arm's length. This feature, unfortunately, is found largely in phones in Korea and Japan. The timer can be set to between 3 and 10 seconds.

▶▶▶ External Card Slot

You can expand the storage capacity of a camera phone by leaps and bounds if it has an external card slot. By using a 128MB card, for instance, you can store up to approximately 1500 images at VGA quality.

▶▶▶ Other Camera Features

Some camera phones have a Night mode which, as the name suggests, is for taking pictures at night. In addition, some camera phones let the user choose a light-metering method.

▶▶▶ Connectivity

There is only one feature of the camera phone that beats the digital cameras hands down, and it is connectivity. With camera phones, it can be so easy to share your images. You can upload your images to a website directly from your phone if your phone has GPRS technology and you have a GPRS subscription. Using MMS-enabled phones, you can also e-mail your pictures to your friends directly from the phone.

Techniques for Taking Pictures with the Camera Phone

In this section, you will learn the techniques for taking pictures and the situations where you cannot expect to get good shots with a camera phone. Because most camera phones have very basic camera capabilities, there are many types of images that you won't be able to capture with a camera phone successfully.

▶▶▶ People Shots

Camera phones are most frequently used for taking close-ups of people, and this is also what camera phones do best. Instead of taking the standard, head-on portrait shots of people, try out different camera angles and occasionally take the pictures in the landscape orientation.

▶▶▶ Lighting

Because most camera phones do not have a flash that is as bright as a camera's, you will not be able to take shots in low-light situations. The shot will be underexposed unless you can increase the ambient lighting by using other light sources such as a lamp.

▶▶▶ Action

Without a flash and fast shutter speed, it is impossible to capture a freeze frame of any moving object when shooting with a camera phone.

▶▶▶ Landscape

Without optical zoom and hampered by low resolution, camera phones cannot capture the details in a landscape. You should avoid taking shots far away from the subject. Another reason for taking close-ups is due to the LCD screen size. Because LCD screens are small, you need to take close-ups for the shape of the subject to show up clearly on-screen. It also helps if the subject has a distinct outline and a color that contrasts with the background.

▶▶▶ Macro Photography

For now, camera phones cannot take a close-up of small objects.

Contents of the Supplementary CD

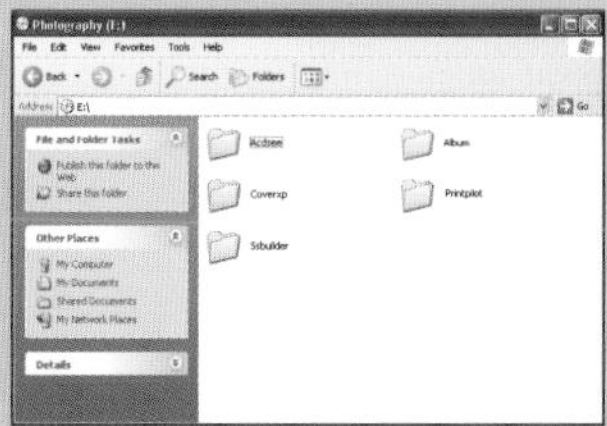

Insert the supplementary CD-ROM in your CD-ROM drive. You should see the folders as shown. All of these programs allow you to do more with your digital images in less time. After the trial period ends, you can choose to buy the Adobe software online or from your local computer store. As for shareware, you can buy it online or from catalogs. Freeware is free of charge.

ACDSee 6.3 [Windows], Trial Version

ACDSee 6.3 allows you to get, view, organize, print, and share your images easily. Double-click on the **acdsee.exe** file in the Acdsee folder to install a tryout version. Website: www.acdsystems.com

Coverxp 1.65 [Windows], Trial Version

You can use coverxp 1.65 to create CD covers for the CD-ROM recordings of your vacations or other special occasions. Double-click on the **cxp_pro165.exe** file in the Coverxp folder to install the free program. Website: www.coverxp.com

Photoshop Album (Windows), Trial Version

You can use Photoshop Album to create an electronic photo album. The software lets you make simple image modifications; organize photos by theme; turn images into slideshows, albums, cards or calendars; and share your photos with others. Double-click on the **psa2se_us.zip** file in the Album folder to extract and create Starter Edition folder. Double-click on the **setup.exe** file in the psa2se_us folder to install a tryout version. Website: www.adobe.com

Print Pilot 1.32 [Windows], Trial Version

Print Pilot 1.32 lets you organize a few digital photos on a single page and print them. This makes printing faster and more convenient for those people who print a lot of graphics, because they will not need to print the images one at a time. Double-click on the **prpil.exe** file in the Printpilot folder to install a tryout version. Website: www.colorpilot.com

Screen Saver Builder 3.30 [Windows], Trial Version

You can use Screen Saver Builder 3.30 to merge your favorite images and photos with sounds and music to create screen savers. Double-click on the **ssbuilder3.exe** file in the Ssbuilder folder to install a tryout version. Website: www.mgshareware.com

Index

A

B

C

D

E

F